American Heritage®
AMERICAN VOICES

COLONIES AND REVOLUTION

David C. King

John Wiley & Sons, Inc.

Published by John Wiley & Sons, Inc., Hoboken, New Jersey
Published simultaneously in Canada

Design and production by Navta Associates, Inc.

American Heritage is a registered trademark of American Heritage Inc. Its use is pursuant to a license agreement.

For general information about our other products and services, please contact our Customer Care Department within the United States at (800) 762-2974, outside the United States at (317) 572-3993 or fax (317) 572-4002.

Wiley also publishes its books in a variety of electronic formats. Some content that appears in print may not be available in electronic books. For more information about Wiley products, visit our web site at www.wiley.com.

Library of Congress Cataloging-in-Publication Data:

King, David C.
   Colonies and revolution / David King.
      p. cm.— (American Heritage, American voices)
   Summary: Presents a picture of life in America prior to and during the American Revolution using excerpts from diaries, advertisements, court proceedings, speeches, and political documents of the day.
   Includes bibliographical references and index.
   Contents: Colonizing a new world — Daily life in colonial America — Many people, many voices — Prelude to revolution — The American Revolution — Creating a national government.
   ISBN 0-471-44391-3 (pbk. : alk. paper)
   1. United States—History—Colonial period, ca. 1600–1775—Sources—Juvenile literature. 2. United States—History—Revolution, 1775–1783—Sources—Juvenile literature. [1. United States—History—Colonial period, ca. 1600–1755—Sources. 2. United States—History—Revolution, 1775–1783—Sources.] I. Title.

E187 .K56 2002
973.—dc21   2002032430

Printed in the United States of America

10 9 8 7 6 5 4 3 2 1

CONTENTS

Introduction to the American Heritage® American Voices Series

For more than four hundred years of our nation's history, Americans have left a long paper trail of diaries, letters, journals, and other personal writings. Throughout this amazingly vast collection, we can often find intriguing information about the events that make up that history. A diary entry, for example, can help us feel we are on the scene, as in this army officer's entry on the eve of a critical Revolutionary War battle: "It is fearfully cold, and a storm setting in. The wind is northeast and beats in the faces of the men. It will be a terrible night for the soldiers who have no shoes."

These firsthand accounts can also present us with surprises. In 1836, for instance Narcissa Whitman was warned that hardship and possibly death awaited her on the rugged Oregon Trail. But from the trail she wrote: "Our manner of living is preferable to any in the States [the East]. I never was so happy and content before. Neither have I enjoyed such health." And personal writings can also take us inside the minds of people caught up in events, as in the case of Clara Barton, who became famous as a battlefield nurse in the Civil War but first had to wrestle with doubts about whether it was proper for a woman to tend wounded soldiers. "I struggled long and hard," she wrote, "with the appalling fact that I was only a woman . . . [but] thundering in my ear were the groans of suffering men dying like dogs [to save the society] that had protected and educated me."

Intriguing fragments like these make up our nation's history. Journals, letters, diaries, and other firsthand accounts are called primary sources. In addition to letters and journals, other voices from the past emerge from newspapers, books, and magazines, from poems and songs, from advertisements, pamphlets, and government documents. Added to the written records are "visual documents" such as sketches, diagrams, patent designs, maps, paintings, engravings, and photographs.

Historians have the fascinating work of sifting through these fragments, searching for the ones that will add a special touch to their reconstruction of the past. But historians are not the only ones who can appreciate these details. America's huge storehouse of primary materials offers a great opportunity to make history more interesting, exciting, and meaningful to everyone. History textbooks are useful for providing the bare bones of history, but firsthand accounts add the muscle and sinew, fleshing out the story with the experiences of real men and women. Primary sources also let you come to your own conclusions about what happened in the past, and they help you make connections between the past and the present.

In creating this series, we've looked for selections that draw out the drama, excitement, tragedy, and humor that have characterized the American experience. The cast of characters comes from a variety of backgrounds and time periods, but they all have authentic American voices, and they have all contributed to our nation's story. We have kept most of the selections short in order to include as many different voices and viewpoints as possible.

The language of primary sources can be difficult, especially material written in the 1600s and 1700s. For this series, we have modernized some of the spelling and grammar so that the texts are easier to understand, while being careful to maintain the meaning and tone of the original. We have also provided vocabulary and background information in the margins to help you understand the texts. For the most part, however, we have let the American voices speak for themselves. We hope that what they have to say will interest you, sometimes surprise you, and even inspire you to learn more about America's history.

Introduction to
Colonies and Revolution

America became a nation at a special time in history—a time when an unusually large number of people were writing about events in their lives and in the world around them. Many of the early American colonists were educated enough to write letters, diaries, and journals. Some wrote about events because they sensed that something special was happening and they wanted to record it; others were just going about their daily business of building a farm or business, raising a family, or perhaps planning to move a little farther into the western wilderness. These informal writings give us valuable clues to how a scattered group of colonies grew to become a strong nation united around the goals of independence and self-government.

In *Colonies and Revolution,* you will encounter some of the people who lived through the very first chapters in our nation's story—from the efforts to establish colonies in the late 1500s to the dramatic moment when George Washington became the first president of the United States. You will read accounts by people in the first settlements of the "starving time," when half the people died within a year. And you will learn what happened when history's first submarine tried to sink a British warship in New York Harbor—in the words of the man who bravely agreed to pilot the sub. You will also read twenty-year-old Deborah Champion's letter describing her dangerous ride to get a message through enemy lines to General Washington.

You will encounter some surprises. Did you know that Paul Revere never completed his famous ride? Or that Benedict Arnold was once considered America's greatest soldier? You may not know that some of the most outspoken patriots, like Patrick Henry, refused to support the Constitution because it created a government that would be too strong.

Peer over the shoulder of a twelve-year-old schoolgirl in colonial Boston as she writes to her mother. Listen to a teenage boy describe his uneasiness about his first Revolutionary War battle. Overhear two patriot leaders joke about the fact that the British could now hang them for treason because they have just signed the Declaration of Independence. Discover America's history from the people who lived it.

PART I

COLONIZING A NEW WORLD

Before Europeans arrived in North America, the continent had been populated for thousands of years by many Native American tribes. Although several explorers from other countries reached North America before Christopher Columbus, historians often say that American history began with Columbus's four voyages from 1492 to 1504, because it was he who first brought together the "Old World" of Europe, Africa, and Asia and the "New World" of the Americas. The birth of the colonies that eventually became the United States can be traced back to Columbus's discovery.

Nearly a century passed after the voyages of Columbus before anyone showed much interest in the part of North America north of what is now Mexico. During that century the Spanish built their mighty New World empire of New Spain, stretching from modern-day Mexico south through most of South

1

America. By the mid-1500s they were sending shiploads of plundered treasure from conquered Indian empires back to Spain and making that nation the envy of Europe. That envy was one reason some European explorers and adventurers became interested in North America. Others hoped to find a waterway through the landmass that would lead them to the wealth of Asia. Gradually, a few people, especially the English and French, decided to try to establish colonies along the Atlantic shores. After the first English colony at Roanoke in Virginia failed, some courageous settlers managed to start a colony at Jamestown, also in Virginia, in 1607, and another at Plymouth in Massachusetts in 1620.

The settlements at both Jamestown and Plymouth barely survived the first years, which became known as the "starving time": more than half the colonists died of disease or starvation. But after those first hard years, both colonies gradually prospered, and a growing number of people made the Atlantic crossing to establish more towns and new colonies. By the early 1700s thirteen English colonies were spread along the Atlantic coast.

Christopher Columbus Signs a Contract

A *primary source,* such as this agreement between Christopher Columbus and the rulers of Spain, provides factual information. From this agreement we learn details about his voyages and discoveries. It also offers information on other subjects, including what Columbus was thinking when he took on his greatest adventure. Columbus was well aware of the risks he was taking in sailing west in the hope of reaching China and the Spice Islands. He might easily have been lost at sea or shipwrecked in a hostile land. He wanted to make sure that, if he survived, he would receive adequate rewards. Before Columbus sailed, his patrons, Queen Isabella and King Ferdinand of Spain, provided him with a document describing the rewards he could expect if he succeeded.

FROM

An Agreement between Christopher Columbus and the Rulers of Spain

APRIL 17, 1492

The things asked for and which your Highnesses grant to Christopher Columbus are as follows:

First, that your Highnesses make, from this time, the said **Don** Christopher Columbus your **Admiral** in all those lands which he shall discover.

Likewise, that your Highnesses make him your **Governor General** in all said lands. . . .

Also, that the said Don Christopher may take the tenth part [10 percent] of all merchandise, whether it be pearls, precious stones, gold, silver, spices, or other things, and give the other nine parts to your Highnesses. . . .

These are **executed** with the responses of your Highnesses in the town of Santa Fe de la Vega de Granada, on the seventeenth of April.

By order of the King and of the Queen

Don is a title of respect, much like "Sir."

admiral: the commander of a fleet of ships.

As **governor general,** Columbus would rule any lands he discovered, second only to the king and queen.

executed: carried out or completed.

Columbus Describes His Voyage

This letter, which Columbus wrote to a friend after his first voyage, describes what he believed he had found. Although he thought he had reached the Indian Ocean, in reality he had explored what are now the Bahamas, Cuba, and Hispaniola. The letter also gives us clues about why all of Europe was thrilled by the news of that voyage. People thought he had found a direct route to the wealth of Asia and had also found people who might be converted to Christianity.

Lord Raphael Sanchez was an official in the court of King Ferdinand and Queen Isabella.

Columbus made three more voyages to the New World. He established a colony but turned out to be a poor governor and treated the people he named "Indians" poorly. He died in 1506, still insisting that the islands he had discovered were just off the coast of China.

pitch: a tar-like substance from pine trees. It was used to make a seal between the boards of a ship for waterproofing.

rhubarb: one of many plants used as medicines.

FROM

Christopher Columbus's Letter to Lord Raphael Sanchez

MARCH 14, 1493

Knowing that it will give you pleasure to learn that I have brought my project to a successful end, I have decided to write you about all the events which occurred on my voyage.

Thirty-three days after my departure, I reached the Indian Sea, where I discovered many islands, thickly populated. I took possession of them in the name of our great King. . . .

In all the islands there is no difference in the physical appearance of the inhabitants or in their manners or language. They all understand each other clearly, a fact which should help our glorious King reach what I assume is his main goal—the conversion of these people to a belief in Christ. . . .

As to the advantages to be gained from my voyage, with a little assistance from our great rulers, I can get them as much gold as they need, as much spice, cotton, and **pitch** as they can use, and as many men for the navy as Their Majesties require. I can bring back **rhubarb** and other kinds of drugs. In fact, I am sure that the men I left in the fort have already found some.

The Mystery of Roanoke

Small numbers of French, Spanish, English, and Portuguese arrived in North America in the 1600s. In 1565 the Spanish established the first permanent settlement in North America, St. Augustine in Florida. In 1584 Queen Elizabeth of England granted Sir Walter Raleigh all of the land he could occupy in what would be called Virginia (after Elizabeth, the

"Virgin Queen"). He sent his first party of settlers to Roanoke, an island off the coast of Virginia, in 1585, but after less than a year they abandoned their settlement and returned to England. In 1587 Raleigh sent a second expedition to Roanoke, this time including women and children. The governor of the colony was John White, who had been along on the first expedition. He was a skilled artist who created an outstanding watercolor record of Indian life at the time. Shortly after the colonists landed, White's daughter Eleanor gave birth to Virginia Dare, the first English child born in North America. But a few weeks after the birth of Virginia Dare, Governor White was forced to head back to England for supplies. He left 117 colonists on Roanoke.

White expected to collect the supplies and return to the Virginia coast in a matter of weeks, but three years passed before he could return. What he found when he got there was that the colony had been deserted. This selection from White's journals briefly describes his search of Roanoke in 1590.

FROM

John White's Journals

1590

We espied toward the north end of the island the light of a great fire [toward] which we rowed. We let go our **grapnel** near the shore and sounded the trumpet a call, and afterwards many familiar English tunes and songs, and called to them friendly. But we had no answer. We therefore landed at daybreak, and coming to the fire, we found the grass and sundry rotten trees burned. . . . We returned to the place where I had left our colony in the year 1587.

. . . As we entered up the sandy bank, upon a tree . . . were curiously carved these fair Roman letters CRO; which letters . . . we knew to signify the place where I should find the colonists seated, according to a secret token agreed upon between them and me . . . , which was that they

grapnel: a hook containing three or four barbs that was attached to a rope. When the grapnel was thrown, the hooks caught in rocks and could be used to anchor a boat or ship.

palisado: a high wall made of logs.

Croatoan: the Indian name of an island near Roanoke. No sign of white colonists, however, was ever found there. It was also the name of an Indian tribe that knew the colonists, but no one can be sure if they had anything to do with the disappearance of the settlers.

should not fail to write or carve on the trees or posts of the doors the name of the place where they should be. . . .

We passed towards the place where they were left in sundry houses, but we found the houses taken down, and the place very strongly enclosed with a high **palisado** of great trees, and one of the chief trees . . . had bark taken off, and five foot from the ground in fair capital letters was graven **CROATOAN**, without any cross or sign of distress.

© COPYRIGHT THE BRITISH MUSEUM

Gray-Eyed Indians

White's story ends here. For some reason, he did not—or could not—continue the search. However, many have since wondered what happened to the missing colonists. Twenty years later settlers at Jamestown were told by Indians in the region that white people had been living among the Native Americans until Chief Powhatan ordered them killed. Seven of the people—four men, two boys, and a young girl—were said to be under the protection of another chief, however, and were spared. About one hundred years later, in the early 1700s, colonists in Carolina reported finding a small tribe of Indians near Hatteras who had gray eyes. Did some of the Roanoke colonists survive and live with a tribe on the mainland and intermarry? No one knows for certain. More evidence would be needed to prove this theory.

John White's watercolor of an Indian chief

The Legend of Pocahontas

The story of Pocahontas, the Indian princess who saved Captain John Smith, is one of America's favorite legends. The information for much of her story comes to us from Captain John Smith's book *The General History of Virginia, New England and the Summer Isles.* Unfortunately, Smith was not a very reliable historian, especially since he is the hero of most of his book. His account of being rescued by Pocahontas makes an interesting story, but historians have debated for years whether it really happened. Note that in these paragraphs from Smith's book he refers to himself in the third person.

A map of Virginia from John Smith's The General History of Virginia, *1624.*

Captain Smith the Author

Captain Smith wrote several books about his adventures in Virginia. In earlier books, he makes no mention of the Pocahontas rescue story. His *The General History of Virginia* was published in 1624, about sixteen years after his rescue. Readers were fascinated by the wealth of detail he provided, including an excellent map and a description of a region he named New England. But many doubted the truth of Smith's accounts of his many extraordinary acts of heroism.

FROM

John Smith's The General History of Virginia

1 6 2 4

At last they brought Captain Smith to Meronocomoco, where was Powhatan, their emperor. Here more than two hundred of those grim people stood wondering at him, as if he had been a monster.

Before a fire upon a seat like a bedstead sat Powhatan. He was covered with a great robe made of raccoon skins with all the tails hanging on it. . . .

At his entrance before the king, all the people gave a great shout. The queen brought him water to wash his hands. Someone else brought him a bunch of feathers instead of a towel to dry them.

Having feasted him in their best manner, they held a long consultation. The conclusion was that two great stones were brought before Powhatan. Then as many as could laid hands upon Captain Smith. They dragged him to the stones and laid his head on them. They were ready with their clubs to beat out his brains.

Pocahontas, the king's dearest daughter, begged them to stop. When they would not, she got his head in her arms and laid her own upon his to save him from death. At this point Powhatan granted that he should live. He would have to make hatchets for the emperor and bells, beads, and copper for his daughter. They thought him as much a master of all occupations as themselves.

Pocahontas the Princess

We do know that Pocahontas was a real person and a princess. She was about twelve years old when she is said to have rescued Smith. After he left, she continued to help the colonists until 1613, when she was taken prisoner. A colonist named John Rolfe obtained permission from Powhatan and from the governor to marry her. (Rolfe had provided the colony with a means of making money when he began to grow West Indies tobacco, which was very popular in England.) Pocahontas took the English name Rebecca, converted to Christianity, and married Rolfe in 1614.

In 1614 Rolfe took Pocahontas to England, where she was received as a royal visitor. She also had a chance to visit with John Smith, whom she hadn't seen in seven years. In 1617 she became ill and died in London just before she was to return to Virginia.

The First Settlements in New England

In the early winter of 1620 a small, sturdy ship called the *Mayflower* made a difficult crossing of the stormy Atlantic. The 102 passengers included 50 men, women, and children who were part of a deeply religious group we call the Pilgrims. They were looking for a place where they could live in peace and worship according to their beliefs. Their disagreements with the Church of England had made them unpopular in England, and their attempt to live in the Netherlands was not successful, leading them to the bold decision to try the New World.

The *Mayflower* was supposed to land north of Jamestown but still in Virginia, where they would be governed by the rules of the Virginia Company. The ship had been blown off course, however, and landed on what is now Cape Cod. Since they were far north of Virginia, the Pilgrims and the other passengers—called "Strangers" by the Pilgrims—had to decide what they should do since they could not practically be governed by the Virginia Company.

The men crowded into the captain's cabin and drew up an agreement known as the "Mayflower Compact," in which they stated their intention to form their own government. The Mayflower Compact did not actually create a government, but it defined government as an agreement, or contract, among the people. This idea of a contract makes the Mayflower Compact one of the early milestones on the road to American democracy.

The original signed copy of the contract has been lost. The version of the compact included here is from the history of the Pilgrims' settlement written by William Bradford, the colony's governor for many years.

FROM

William Bradford's History of Plymouth Plantation, *"The Mayflower Compact"*

1620—1647

In the name of God, Amen.

We the undersigned, the loyal subjects of our dread sovereign lord, King James . . . , having undertaken for the glory of God and the advancement of the Christian faith and the honor of our king and country a voyage to establish the first colony in the northern part of Virginia, do by this document solemnly and mutually in the presence of God and one another **covenant** and combine ourselves together into a civil political body for ordering and preserving ourselves better and for furthering the above purposes; and on the basis of this compact to enact, constitute, and frame such just and equal laws, ordinances, acts, constitutions, and offices from time to time as shall be thought most proper and convenient for the general good of the Colony, to which we promise all proper submission and obedience. In witness of which we have signed our names to this compact at Cape Cod on the 11th of November . . . 1620.

covenant: to pledge.

$\mathcal{T}$he Survival of Plymouth Plantation

After first landing at Cape Cod on November 21, 1620, the Pilgrims moved to Plymouth on the coast of present-day Massachusetts. Within weeks the settlers encountered what became known as the "starving time." Half the company died from starvation, exposure, and diseases like scurvy. The survivors managed to get through that first year thanks not only to their own determination and courage but to help from Squanto, a Pawtuxet Indian living with the Wampanoag tribe. Squanto, who could speak English, taught the colonists how to grow corn, squash, and beans; how to fish; and how to dig for clams. By autumn they had an abundance of food, including deer, turkey, and a variety of migrating waterfowl. The selection below is an account of the starving time from William Bradford's diary. The Pilgrims' first feast of thanksgiving was held only about seven months after that first hard winter.

F R O M

William Bradford's History of Plymouth Plantation

1 6 2 0 – 1 6 4 7

Soon a most lamentable blow fell upon them. In two or three months' time half of their company died, partly owing to the severity of the winter, especially during January and February, and the want of houses and other comforts; partly from scurvy and other diseases, which their long voyage and their **incommodious** quarters had brought upon them. Of all the hundred odd persons, scarcely fifty remained, and sometimes two or three persons died in a day. In the time of worst distress, there were but six or seven **sound** persons, who, to their great commendation be it spoken, spared no pains night or day, but with great toil and at the risk of their own health, fetched wood, made fires, prepared food for the sick, made their beds, washed their infected clothes, dressed and undressed them—in a word, did all the homely and necessary services for them which dainty and queasy stomachs cannot endure to hear mentioned; and all this they did willingly and cheerfully, showing their love to their friends and their brethern; a rare example and worthy to be remembered.

Why Plymouth *Plantation*? Every new settlement was called a plantation.

incommodious: inconvenient.

sound: healthy.

Two of these seven were Mr. William Brewster, their reverend elder, and Myles Standish, their captain and military commander, to whom myself and many others were much beholden in our low and sick condition. And yet the Lord so upheld these men that in this general calamity they were not at all infected with sickness. And what I have said of these few, I should say of many others who died in this general visitation, and others yet living, that while they had health and strength, they forsook none that had need of them. I doubt not that their **recompense** is with the Lord.

recompense: reward.

Mosquito Warning

They are too delicate and unfitte to begine new plantations and colonies that cannot enduer the biting of a muskeato; we would wish such to keepe at home till at least they be muskeato proofe.

—from Bradford's *History of Plymouth Plantation*

AMERICAN HERITAGE PUBLISHING CO., INC.

Sketch of Plymouth in 1627.

About Squanto

Squanto was a member of the Pawtuxet tribe who had been taken prisoner by an English sea captain some years earlier. He found his way back to New England, probably with the help of Captain John Smith, but his village had been wiped out by an epidemic of smallpox. Smallpox was until that time only a European disease. The Indians' bodies had no defenses against smallpox, which became a major reason for the decline of Native American populations after the arrival of Europeans.

A Difficult Voyage

From the moment a family of colonists stepped aboard the ship that would carry them to the New World, they faced a series of risks, including storms, hunger, disease, and shipwreck. It has been estimated that one out of every ten who started out never made it across the Atlantic. The voyage normally took four to six weeks, but storms frequently stretched the time to ten weeks or more. In the next selection, you'll read about a German immigrant's terrifying voyage in 1750. He returned home as soon as he could.

FROM

A German Immigrant's Letter Home

1750

The ship was full of pitiful signs of distress—smells, fumes, horrors, vomiting, various kinds of sea sickness, fever, **dysentery,** headaches, constipation, boils, scurvy, **mouth-rot,** and similar afflictions—all of them caused by the age and the highly salted state of the food, especially of the meat, as well as by the bad and very filthy water, which brings about the

dysentery: a very serious form of diarrhea.

mouth-rot: blackening of the mouth and loss of teeth caused by scurvy.

miserable [sickness] and death of many. Add to all that the shortage of food, hunger, thirst, frost, heat, dampness, fear, misery, **vexation** . . . as well as other troubles. . . .

All this misery reached its climax when . . . one must suffer through two or three days and nights of storm, with everyone convinced that the ship with all aboard is bound to sink. In such misery, all the people on board pray and cry pitifully. . . . Many groan and exclaim, "Oh! If only I were back at home, even lying in my pigsty!"

vexation: distress.

The Scourge of Scurvy

Scurvy was a common disease in the 1600s, especially among people who spent long periods at sea. The victim of scurvy found his mouth turning black and his teeth falling out. Bleeding was also common, from the mouth and under the surface of the skin. Unless treated, the patient died.

In the 1730s a Scottish naval doctor found that citrus fruits, such as oranges, lemons, and limes, produced a nearly miraculous cure. These provided the vitamins A and C, which the body needed—although no one at the time knew what vitamins were. News of the cure for scurvy spread rapidly. Scurvy remained a problem on land, especially among the very poor and during the winter months in the North, when people often ate unbalanced meals. As a protection against scurvy, colonial families tried to have citrus fruits on hand all the time even though they were usually expensive.

Keeping a Sense of Humor

Most colonists learned to put up with the hardships—not just of the crossing but the first months in their new home as well. The New England settlers had to deal with a climate that was far harsher than Old England. They learned to rely on hearty, plain foods that could be stored for months, such as pumpkins and root vegetables, including carrots and turnips. The lyrics of the following song suggest that a sense of humor was another one of their aids to survival.

Forefathers' Song

c. 1630

New England's annoyances, you that would know them,
Pray ponder these verses which briefly doth show them.
The place where we live is a wilderness wood,
Where grass is much wanting that's fruitful and good;
Our mountains and hills and our valleys below,
Being commonly covered with ice and with snow;
And when the north-west wind with violence blows
Then every man pulls his cap over his nose;
But if any's so hardy and will it withstand,
He forfeits a finger, a foot or a hand.

But when the Spring opens we then take the hoe,
And make the ground ready to plant and to sow;
Our corn being planted and seed being sown,
The worms destroy much before it is grown;
And when it is growing, some spoil there is made
By birds and by squirrels that pluck up the blade;
And when it is come to full corn in the ear,
It is often destroyed by raccoon and by deer. . . .

If fresh meat be wanting to fill up our dish,
We have carrots and turnips as much as we wish;
And if there's a mind for a delicate dish
We repair to the clam-banks, and there we catch fish.

Instead of **pottage** and puddings and custards and pies,
Our pumpkins and parsnips are common supplies.
We have pumpkins at morning and pumpkins at noon,
If it was not for pumpkins we should be undone!

pottage: a thick soup, like a stew.

If barley be wanting to make into malt,
We must be contented, and think it no fault.

For we can make liquor to sweeten our lips,
Of pumpkins and parsnips and walnut-tree chips. . . .
But you whom the Lord intends hither to bring,
Forsake not the honey for fear of the sting,
But bring both a quiet and contented mind,
And all needful blessings you surely will find.

Indenture: Encouraging Newcomers

Many people in England and other European countries wanted to migrate to the colonies, but they had no money to pay for passage on a ship. One solution was to sign an *indenture*—a contract stating that you would agree to work for a period of years (usually seven) for the person who would pay the fee. The system was successful because many established colonists wanted workers or household servants. In addition, business owners were pleased by the arrival of every ship bringing new colonists because a growing population meant increased business activity. The next reading is the agreement signed by Aulkey Hubertse, a Dutch girl, in 1710, making her an indentured servant.

Aulkey Hubertse's Indenture Contract

1 7 1 0

This indenture witnesses that Aulkey Hubertse of Rensse-laerwyck, daughter of the [dead] John Hubertse, has bound herself as a house servant. She has of her own free will bound herself as a house servant to John Delemont, a weaver of the City of Albany. The deacons of the Reformed Dutch Church have given their consent. She will serve from the date of these present indentures [1710] until she shall come of age.

During this term the servant shall serve her master faithfully. She shall keep his secrets and gladly obey his lawful commands. She shall do no damage to her master nor see it done by others without telling her master. She shall not waste her master's goods, nor lend them unlawfully to anyone.

And the master, during the term, shall provide enough meat and drink, washing, lodging, and clothing. He shall also provide all other necessities fit for such a servant.

It is further agreed between the master and servant that in case Aulkey Hubertse should marry before she shall come of age, then the servant is free from her service.

At the end of her service, John Delemont shall deliver to the servant clothes fit for wearing on the Lord's Day as well as on working days. This includes both linen and woolen stockings and shoes and other necessities. For the true performance of all and every part of this agreement, the two parties bind themselves to each other.

Indentured Servant or Slave?

Until the early 1700s some indentured servants were treated more like slaves than as servants or apprentices. Labor was in such short supply that landowners would accept the indentures of children who were kidnapped in England. An estimated twenty thousand English convicts were *transported* (a system in which prisoners were sent to overseas colonies) to the "Tobacco Coast" (Virginia, parts of Maryland, and North Carolina) to empty the prisons. Some convicts were given the opportunity to escape execution by signing a fourteen-year indenture. A 1666 report showed that more than half of Virginia's population were, or had been, indentured servants. Many of these Tobacco Coast servants labored under harsh conditions, with poor food and shelter. As England became more prosperous in the early 1700s fewer people were willing to sign indentures, and landowners in the South turned to buying slaves from Africa.

Pennsylvania: Drawing Colonists from the Continent

The indenture system provided one way to bring more settlers to England's colonies. The English also developed a new kind of colony called a *proprietary colony*. In this system, a friend of the king—or several friends—were granted a tract of land in North America. The proprietors then owned the colony and were responsible for governing it.

In 1664 King Charles II agreed to let several men become proprietors of a colony, which they named Carolina in honor of the king. In addition to Carolina, Charles II granted New York to his brother, the Duke of York, and friends of the duke became proprietors of New Jersey. Another large tract was given to William Penn to repay a debt to Penn's father, one of the king's admirals.

Penn named his colony Pennsylvania, meaning "Penn's Woods," and he wanted it to become a haven for people of all nations and religions. Penn had his agents travel throughout the continent of Europe, distributing pamphlets and visiting churches. This approach attracted many who migrated from the states of Germany. Pennsylvania, established in 1680, grew rapidly and was soon one of the most populous of all the colonies, with a large percentage of non-English settlers. The following selection is from one of Penn's promotional pamphlets.

The Quakers

Penn was a member of a religious sect called Quakers, or the Society of Friends, which originated in England in the 1650s. The Quakers believed that Jesus Christ was the only religious authority and that Christ spoke directly to each individual human heart. This belief threatened the leaders of the established church, who accused the Quakers of blasphemy. Quakers were also pacifists, even refusing military service. They were frequently in trouble with the authorities in England and in Puritan Boston, and were sometimes thrown in jail. Penn himself had once been imprisoned in the Tower of London.

F R O M

William Penn's Some Further Account of the Province of Pennsylvania in America

1 6 8 3

The people are a collection of different nations in Europe, such as French, Dutch, Germans, Swedes, Danes, Finns,

Scots, Irish, and English. But as they are of one kind and in one place and under one allegiance, so they live like people of one country. . . .

During the first ten months since our arrival we had got up 80 houses at our town, and some villages were settled about it. During the next year the town advanced to 357 houses. Many of them were large and well-built, with good cellars and three stories. Some had balconies.

There is also a fair wharf of about three hundred square feet. . . .

There lived most sorts of useful tradespeople such as carpenters, bricklayers, masons, plasterers, plumbers, smiths, glaziers, tailors, shoemakers, butchers, bakers, tanners, shipwrights. . . .

The hours for work and meals to laborers are fixed and known by ring of bell.

Penn's "Holy Experiment"

Penn called his colony a "Holy Experiment," not only for its religious toleration, but also because of his treatment of the Indians. Unlike other proprietors, he signed treaties with the various tribes and paid them for the land the king had granted him. Pennsylvania was spared the Indian wars that were waged in the other colonies.

One of America's early artists, the Quaker preacher Edward Hicks, painted many versions of *The Peaceable Kingdom* showing Penn meeting with one of the tribes.

WORCESTER ART MUSEUM, WORCESTER, MASSACHUSETTS

The Peaceable Kingdom, *an oil painting by Edward Hicks, c. 1833. William Penn and the Indians appear on the left in the background.*

PART II

DAILY LIFE IN COLONIAL AMERICA

Throughout America's early colonial years, more than 90 percent of the people lived on small family-owned farms. There were no tractors or other farm machines. Work was performed with hand tools, often aided by the power supplied by a horse or a pair of oxen. An average family produced enough for its own needs, with some left over to sell or or trade for things they could not produce themselves, such as salt, gunpowder, glass for windows, and shoes or boots.

After the hard beginnings of the earliest settlements, the colonists achieved a surprising level of prosperity within a generation. By the early 1700s farms were producing enough surpluses to feed rapidly growing villages and towns. More and more people could support themselves with a craft or trade. Farm families still made most of their own clothing and other household items, but most could afford to purchase at least an occasional item from a craftsperson, such as a dressmaker, cabinetmaker, gunsmith, or potter. Some of the farm family's children could sign on as apprentices to a craftsperson with the hope of entering the craft and living in town.

In New England the rocky soil and short growing season made farming much more difficult than in the Middle Colonies or the South. This led many young men to turn to the sea for their livelihood. By 1750 more than ten thousand New Englanders lived by fishing, whaling, shipbuilding, or trade.

By 1732, when Georgia was established, there were thirteen English colonies along the Atlantic coast. Each colony had its own *assembly,* or legislature, elected by male property owners or, in New England, members of the church, and a governor, either elected or appointed by the king. While the colonial assemblies made most of a colony's laws, the final authority over the colonies was the English king and the *Parliament,* England's legislative body. Through the 1600s and the first half of the 1700s the king and Parliament allowed the colonies to manage their own affairs in most matters.

*A*ll in a Day's Work

Everyone in a farm family worked hard, usually performing a variety of tasks every day. In addition to the farmwork, the labor involved in preparing meals and preserving food must have seemed endless. Older farm children worked nearly as hard as their parents. The selection below is from a thirteen-year-old girl's description in her diary of one day's activities.

short thread: linen was made in short and long threads; the long was used for a rougher form of linen called *tow.*

carded: wool, cotton, or linen thread was wound onto cards or onto round spools.

hetchel'd: one of the stages in making linen out of flax.

FROM

A Girl's Diary

1775

Fixed gown for Prue,—Mend Mother's Riding-hood, Spun **short thread,**—Fix'd two gowns for Welsh's girl,—**Carded** tow,—Spun linen,—Worked on Cheese-basket,—**Hetchel'd** flax with Hannah, we did 51 lbs. apiece,—Pleated and ironed,—Read a Sermon of Dodridge's,—Spooled a piece—Milked the Cows,—Spun linen, did 50 knots,—Made a Broom of Guinea wheat straw,—Spun thread to whiten,—Set a Red dye,—I carded two pounds of whole wool and felt,—Spun harness twine,—Scoured the pewter,—Ellen was **spark'd** last night,—spun thread to whiten—Went to Mr. Otis's and made them a **swinging visit**—Israel said I might ride his **jade**.

spark'd: sparked, or courted.

swinging visit: a brief, informal visit.

jade: a horse.

Life in Williamsburg

In 1759 and 1760 an Englishman named Andrew Burnaby made an extensive tour of the colonies. He kept a detailed journal of his wanderings, noting jealousies among the different settlements as well as those things that tended to unite them. In the following excerpt, he gives his impressions of Williamsburg, the Virginia town that was the seat of the colony's government. Burnaby's *Travels Through the Middle Settlements in North America* was not published until 1775, on the eve of the American Revolution.

FROM

Andrew Burnaby's Travels . . .

1759

Williamsburg is the capital of Virginia. It consists of about 200 houses, and does not contain more than 1,000 people, whites and Negroes. It is far from being a place of any real importance.

Upon the whole, it is a pleasant place to live. There are ten or twelve gentlemen's families constantly living in it, besides merchants and tradesmen. At the time of the assemblies and general courts, it is crowded with the upper class of the country, the planters. On those occasions there are balls and other amusements. But as soon as the business of the court and assembly is finished, the people return to their plantations and the town is nearly deserted.

The trade of this colony is large and extensive. Tobacco is the main thing traded. Of this they export each year between 50 and 60 thousand hogsheads, each weighing 800 or 1,000 pounds.

From what has been said of this colony [Virginia], it will not be difficult to get an idea of what the people are like. The climate and nature of this country make them lazy, easy-going, and good-natured. They are extremely fond of each other's company, and of eating and drinking together. They seldom show any ambition or become tired from hard work.

Their public life is like their private life. They are jealous of their liberties, and can hardly stand the idea of being controlled by any superior power. Many of them consider the colonies as independent states, not connected with Great Britain, except by having the same common king. There are but few of them interested in business.

Upon the whole, however, to do them justice, they have a spirit of generosity. They are loyal and never refuse any necessary supplies for the support of government when called upon.

Education and Morals

Education was very uneven throughout the colonies. In New England every town was required to hire a schoolteacher. Boys—and girls in some towns—attended school for a few weeks in the winter, when there was less need for their farmwork. In more prosperous communities there were also private schools, although many families preferred to educate their daughters at home. Girls of all social classes learned "domestic arts," like spinning, weaving, sewing, and embroidery, and farm girls learned such skills as preserving foods, making dairy products, and dying cloth.

In the Middle Colonies numerous schools were established by various religious groups, such as the Quakers. Philadelphia and New York also offered private schools, as well as specialized schools for music, dancing, and art. There were few schools in the South, but plantation owners provided tutors for their children.

This selection is from *The New England Primer*, one of the few schoolbooks used in the schools of New England. It was written by Benjamin Harris, a Puritan minister, probably about 1680. Often called the "Little Bible," it combined lessons in grammar and spelling with religious teaching.

FROM

The New England Primer

C. 1680

In **A**dam's fall
We sinned all.

Thy life to mend
This **B**ook attend.

The **C**at doth play
And after slay.

A **D**og will bite
A thief at night.

An **E**agle's flight
Is out of sight.

The idle **F**ool
Is whipt at school.

As runs the **G**lass
  [hourglass]
Man's life doth pass.

My book and **H**eart
Shall never part.

Job feels the rod,
Yet blesses God.

Kings should be good;
Not men of blood.

The **L**ion bold
The Lamb doth hold.

The **M**oon gives light
In time of night.

Nightingales sing
In time of Spring.

Young **O**badias, David,
  Josias,
All were pious.

Peter denies
His Lord, and cries.

Queen Esther sues,
And saves the Jews.

Rachel doth mourn
For her first-born.

Samuel anoints
Whom God appoints.

Time cuts down all
Both great and small.

Uriah's beauteous wife
Made David seek his life.

Whales in the sea
God's voice obey.

Xerxes the Great did die
And so must you and I.

Youth forward slips;
Death sooner nips.

Zaccheus he
Did climb the tree
His Lord to see.

In *Adam*'s Fall
We finned all.

Thy Life to mend
This Book attend.

The Cat doth play
And after flay.

A Dog will bite
A Thief at Night.

The Eagle's Flight
Is out of Sight.

The idle Fool
Is whipt at School.

Page from The New England Primer, *1769.*

The School of Good Manners, 1675

This was another popular book for teaching young children. Here is a sample of the rules it advocated: "Never speak to thy parents without some title of respect, as, Sir, Madam. . . . Go not out of doors without thy parents' leave, and return within the time by them limited. . . . Quarrel not nor contend with thy brothers or sisters, but live in love, peace, & unity. . . . Bear with meekness & patience, and without murmuring or sullenness, thy parents' reproofs or corrections."

Washington's Rules for Civil Behavior

George Washington, who went on to become the first president of the United States, wrote a book about civility when he was fourteen years old. He borrowed many ideas from another book of rules of behavior to create his own book of 110 rules, or *maxims,* to study.

FROM
George Washington's
Rules of Civility & Decent
Behaviour

1747

Every action done in company ought to be with some sign of respect to those that are present.

If you cough, sneeze, sigh, or yawn, do it not loud but privately; and speak not in your yawning, but put your handkerchief—or hand before your face and turn aside.

When you sit down, keep your feet firm and even, without putting one on the other or crossing them.

Show not yourself glad at the misfortune of another, though he be your enemy.

Superfluous compliments and all affectation of ceremony are to be avoided.

Do not laugh too much or too loud in public.

Clothing in the Age of Homespun

Throughout the colonial period most Americans lived by farming, and each family made most of its own clothing. The styles were simple and practical. Men usually wore a loose linen shirt, a vest, and breeches that reached to the knees, with long stockings and shoes with a buckle or boots for field work. Around 1700 soft deerskin became the favorite fabric for vests and breeches. Leather aprons were worn by many craftsmen and by tradesmen such as millers and blacksmiths. As the following selection indicates, many rural colonists were quite pleased with their "homespun" clothing.

FROM

Reverend John Schuyler's Journal

c. 1805

Growing up on a middling farm in New York's Hudson River Valley, nearly all of the clothing we wore was made by hand by my mother, with help from all seven children. We grew our own flax for linen, raised sheep for wool, and traded for a little cotton. Whatever the material, hours of labour were required to transform it into the clothing we called "homespun."

Flax was by far the most troublesome. There were some twenty steps to turn it into linen thread, and each step was slow and difficult. Even soaking the plants after harvesting required the building of a special "steep-pool" for soaking that had to be separate from the stream because the rotting leaves poisoned fish. [After hours spent with such tools as] the flax brake, swingling knives, and hetchels, we ended up with what looked like a pitiful amount of good fibre. But then there was the surprise of how this fibre produced a remarkably large amount of fine linen thread. . . . [Wool and cotton presented other difficulties.]

After all that labour, and our mother's excellent work in weaving and cutting pieces of fabric, I will always remember the good feelings that came with putting on a soft new linen shirt. The girls, too, looked quite fine and, as I recall, each had four different gowns, plus a special one for Sundays and Occasions. These latter were decorated with bits of store-bought lace, or a colorful scarf. Our shoes and hats were also purchased in town. . . . All in all, I believe all of us were proud to be dressed in homespun, and we felt we were as fashionable as we needed to be.

Wealth and Fashion

By the 1700s many merchants, lawyers, and other members of the middle classes could afford to dress nearly as well as the wealthiest Americans. The following short selection is a description of Madame Sarah Knight, a fairly wealthy widow who traveled alone on horseback from Boston to New York City in 1704.

A Description of Dress

1710

Debby looked with curious admiring eyes at the new comer's costume, the scarlet cloak and little round cap of Lincoln green, the puffed and ruffled sleeves, the petticoat of green-drugget cloth, the high heeled leather shoes, with their green ribbon bows, and the **riding mask** of black velvet which Debby remembered to have heard, only ladies of the highest gentility wore.

riding masks: masks worn by stylish upper-class women of the time while riding horses to protect their faces from the elements.

Late-eighteenth-century attire in Europe.

The Salem Witch Trials

For six months in 1692 fear swept through the Massachusetts town of Salem. It began when several girls began having mysterious "fits" in which they shrieked and writhed in pain. The girls eventually accused other villagers of being witches and casting spells on them. The panic spread to everyone in Salem and even other towns as people feared either being attacked by witches or being accused of witchcraft. Several hundred people had been accused, and nearly 150 remained in prison, when the hysteria suddenly ended. Nineteen people were convicted on no more evidence than the accusations of other townspeople and were hanged as witches. Others died in prison. Another victim, a man who refused to answer questions, was "pressed" to death from heavy stones piled on his chest.

Witchcraft trials had been fairly common in Europe since the Middle Ages, and there had been several trials in different parts of New England earlier in the 1600s. Salem was different, however, because the fear it generated gripped the entire community as well as other towns for months.

What happened to create this mass witch hysteria? Some historians have concluded that New England's Puritan ministers felt that they were losing their hold over the people. By encouraging the panic begun by the girls, the ministers were showing the people that they were badly needed to help judges determine guilt or innocence. Another factor in Salem was the role played by a slave from the West Indies named Tituba. Tituba filled the young girls' heads with stories of witches, using a mixture of African, West Indian, and European folklore. This garbled information enabled the girls to describe things in ways that convinced many people that they must have had contact with a witch. Contributing to the spread of the hysteria was the practice of letting an accused witch escape a death sentence by confessing and naming other witches.

By the autumn of 1692 it became obvious to

The Work of Witches

The girls who were responsible for triggering the hysteria testified that the accused were hurting them by some invisible means. They said the witches were pinching them on the arms or sticking them with sharp objects, and that this was what caused them to cry out, sometimes rolling on the floor and shrieking.

The testimony of Tituba and others also included stories of being attacked by creatures, such as a red and black rat, or of flying from place to place on a broom. Some of the wilder stories recounted meetings with the devil, who could take different forms. Witches were also accused of making spells, so someone who had been overheard talking to himself or muttering was likely to be accused of being a witch.

most people in the town that the hysteria was out of control when some began accusing prominent people of witchcraft, including the wife of the governor. Suddenly people could see how preposterous the whole episode was, and the trials abruptly ended.

This reading is from the transcript of the trial of Sarah Good. Good was a poor beggar woman who was one of the first to be accused.

One of the witnesses who testified against Sarah Good was her own four-year-old daughter, Dorcus, who had confessed to being a witch herself. Dorcus spent several months in prison.

FROM

The Transcript of the Trial of Sarah Good

1692

(H)   Sarah Good what evil spirit have you familiarity with.

(SG)   None.

(H)   Have you made no contracte with the devil.

[Good answered no.]

(H)   Why doe you hurt these children.

(g)   I doe not hurt them. I scorn it.

(H)   Who doe you imploy then to doe it.

(g)   I employ no body.

(H)   What creature do you imploy then.

(g)   no creature but I am falsely accused.

(H)   Why did you go away muttering from Mr Parris his house.

(g)   I did not mutter but I thanked him for what he gave my child.

(H)   have you made no contract with the devil.

(g)   no.

[More testimony followed in the same vein. A death warrant was issued July 19, 1692, and Sarah Good was duly executed.]

"H" stands for John Hathorne, one of the judges at the trials. Hathorne's great-great-grandson was the author Nathaniel Hawthorne. Hawthorne added the "w" to his name because of his shame over John Hathorne's role in the trials.

Judge Sewall's Apology

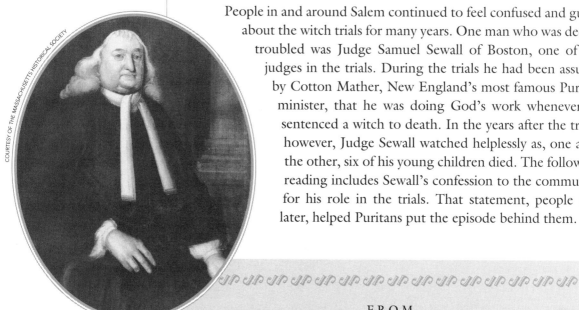

COURTESY OF THE MASSACHUSETTS HISTORICAL SOCIETY

People in and around Salem continued to feel confused and guilty about the witch trials for many years. One man who was deeply troubled was Judge Samuel Sewall of Boston, one of the judges in the trials. During the trials he had been assured by Cotton Mather, New England's most famous Puritan minister, that he was doing God's work whenever he sentenced a witch to death. In the years after the trials, however, Judge Sewall watched helplessly as, one after the other, six of his young children died. The following reading includes Sewall's confession to the community for his role in the trials. That statement, people said later, helped Puritans put the episode behind them.

Portrait of Judge Samuel Sewall by Nathaniel Emmons.

Judge Sewall was the only one of the nine judges who confessed his wrong-doing.

Samuel Sewall was a successful merchant and after his time as a judge was head of the colony's highest court for several years. He was also one of America's great diarists. He kept his diary from 1674 until 1729, a few months before he died— a total of fifty-five years.

FROM

Judge Samuel Sewall's Diary

1696 AND 1697

December 25, 1696

. . . We bury our little daughter. Another of God's strokes of punishment. I went at noon to see in what order things were set; and there [had] a view of . . . the coffins of my six children. . . . I know now what I must do to make some ammends for my sins.

January 14, 1697

I asked the General Court to proclaim this a day of forgiveness and reconciliation. Pastor Willard kindly read the following statement to the assemblage, whilst I stood trembling, with head bowed.

[Read by Pastor Willard as written by Samuel Sewall]

Samuel Sewall, sensible of the reiterated strokes of God upon himself and family; and being sensible that as to the guilt contracted . . . at Salem he is, upon many accounts, . . .

[responsible and] desires to take the blame and shame of it, asking pardon of men, and especially desiring prayers that God, who has an unlimited authority, would pardon that sin.

In 1700 Judge Sewall issued one of the first public statements against slavery. He believed that hiring more indentured servants would be healthier for all.

Anne Bradstreet: America's First Poet

Anne Bradstreet was with the first group of Puritans who established Massachusetts Bay Colony in 1630. She was eighteen years old and had already been married for two years to Simon Bradstreet. Anne's parents, Thomas and Dorothy Dudley, were also in that pioneering group. Her father saw to her education, and both her parents encouraged her interest in writing poetry.

Anne Bradstreet's "To My Dear and Loving Husband"

1678

If ever two were one, then surely we.
If ever man were loved by wife, then thee;
If ever wife was happy in a man,
Compare with me ye women if you can.
I prize thy love more than whole mines of gold,
Or all the riches that the East doth hold.
My love is such that rivers cannot **quench,**
Nor ought but love from thee give **recompense.**
Thy love is such I can no way repay;
The heavens reward thee **manifold,** I pray.
Then while we live, in love let's so **persever,**
That when we live no more we may live ever.

quench: to satisfy a thirst.

recompense: to pay in return.

manifold: in many different ways.

persever: to continue.

The first years in the New World were hard for Anne, but as the towns grew and the farms prospered she grew to love it. Both her father and her husband served as governor of the colony.

Somehow Anne Bradstreet managed to write poetry while raising eight children. Her brother-in-law took some of her poems to England in 1650, where they were published, making her the first published American poet.

Eliza's Gift to South Carolina

Eliza Lucas Pinckney (1722–1793) was one of the most remarkable women in American history. In 1739, when she was seventeen years old, her father was forced to leave the family for two years of military service with the British in the West Indies. He left Eliza in charge of the family's three plantations near Charleston, South Carolina. She also cared for her invalid mother.

Eliza loved the challenge of the work and spent as much time as she could experimenting with plants. She wanted to find another cash crop for South Carolina, which had already been successful in producing rice.

The Remarkable Pinckneys

In 1744 Eliza married a wealthy lawyer and plantation owner, Charles Pinckney. Of their four children, two played important roles in the shaping of the American nation. Charles Cotesworth Pinckney served under General George Washington in the American Revolution and rose to the rank of major general. He was a delegate at the Constitutional Convention in 1787 and later served as a diplomat. His younger brother Thomas also served in the Revolutionary War and later became a major general in the War of 1812. He also served as a diplomat and, in addition, was governor of South Carolina. Both brothers were candidates for vice president of the United States (at different times), and Charles twice lost a bid to become president, in 1800 and 1804.

After dozens of failed experiments, she developed a brand of indigo that could survive the blistering summer heat. Indigo was used to make a deep blue dye—a favored hue throughout the colonies and in Europe. By 1745 South Carolina was exporting one million pounds of indigo a year, and it had become the valuable crop the colony needed.

The following selection is from one of Eliza's many letters to friends.

FROM

A Letter by Eliza Lucas

1740

We are about seventeen miles by land and six by water from Charles Town [later Charleston]. We have about six agreeable families around us with whom we live in great harmony. I have a little library in which I spend part of my time. My music and the garden, which I am very fond of, take up the rest that is not employed in business. Of that my father left me a pretty good share, and indeed 'twas unavoidable. . . .

I have the business of three plantations to transact, which requires much writing and more business (and fatigue of other sorts) than you can imagine. . . . Much of my time is spent on my experiments with indigo—the plant which produces such a beautiful blue dye. . . . I have also taken pains to bring the ginger [and] cotton . . . to perfection [but] have greater hopes from indigo (if I could have the seed earlier next year from the West Indies I would have greater success).

Before her experiments with indigo, Eliza had tried to develop cash crops from ginger, cotton, and alfalfa. After her marriage to Charles Pinckney, she lived on his plantation, where she continued her work with plants. She revived the cultivation of silkworms, which had been tried unsuccessfully in Georgia, and developed a small silk industry.

Advice on Choosing a Husband

Even in the colonial period young women wrote to magazines looking for answers to their questions about romance. The following letter, written by a young woman of seventeen, appeared in the *Royal American Magazine*.

FROM

The Royal American Magazine

1774

. . . [I] am courted by a young gentleman who has no accomplishment or qualification in my eyes . . . [except that he is rich]. My parents insist on my marrying him; and I really think he loves me; but . . . I never can like him; and besides there is a person of whom I am very fond . . . but has . . . [less money]. . . . Now, as I could wish to marry the first for his money, and the last for the love I have [for] him, as well as [his good sense] . . . : In these cases, what shall I do?

[A month later the magazine published this reply:] "The Road before you here is very plain. . . . Follow your Heart and you cannot go wrong."

Advice on Being Feminine

Colonial men accepted some variety in women's roles, but most seemed to be in agreement on two points: first, women should not spend too much time on intellectual pursuits; and second, women should avoid political debate. These attitudes would continue through much of American history. In 1645 Governor Winthrop of the Massachusetts Bay

Colony wrote of the sad case of a woman who appeared to him to have lost her wits from too much reading and writing.

FROM

John Winthrop's
History of New England

1 6 4 5

Mr. Hopkins, the governor of Hartford upon Connecticut, came to Boston and brought his wife with him (a godly young woman, and of special parts), who was fallen into a sad infirmity, the loss of her understanding and reason, which had been growing upon her divers years, by occasion of her giving herself wholly to reading and writing, and had written many books. If she had attended to her household affairs, and such things as belong to women, and not gone out of her way and calling to meddle in such things as are proper for men, whose minds are stronger, etc., she had kept her wits, and might have improved them usefully and honorably in the place God had set her.

Living Well

By 1750 Americans were enjoying a standard of living that was probably higher than anywhere in Europe, perhaps anywhere in the world. From the difficult beginnings at Jamestown and Plymouth, the population of the colonies had grown to more than one million people by the mid-1700s. Many of these people were living very well in the towns and on plantations.

The following excerpts from the diary of John Adams, who became the second president of the United States, give some indication of the plenty enjoyed by the well-to-do. Note that Adams was describing *three* separate meals, enjoyed within a few days of each other.

plain: a common Quaker term, by which they meant simple (in a pleasant way).

fools: desserts made with crushed fruit and cream or custard.

trifles: desserts typically including cake, liquor, jam, fruit, custard, and whipped cream.

floating islands: a soft custard with beaten egg whites or whipped cream floating on the surface.

flummery: a light, sweet, bland mixture of milk and flour, like a pudding.

sweetmeats: candies.

sillabub or **syllabyb:** a drink made with wine or liquor mixed with cream.

FROM

The Diary of John Adams

1775

[At the home of Miers Fisher, a young Quaker lawyer]

This **plain** Friend, . . . with his plain but pretty wife with her Thees and Thous, had provided us a costly entertainment; ducks, hams, chickens, beef, pig, tarts, creams, custards, jellies, **fools, trifles, floating islands,** beer, porter, punch, wine and a long, etc.

[At the home of Chief Justice Chew]

About four o'clock we were called to dinner. Turtle and every other thing, **flummery,** jellies, **sweetmeats** of twenty sorts, trifles, whipped **sillabubs,** floating islands, fools, etc., with a dessert of fruits, raisins, almonds, pears, peaches.

A most sinful feast again! Everything which could delight the eye or allure the taste; curds and creams, jellies, sweetmeats of various sorts, twenty kinds of tarts, fools, trifles, floating islands, whipped sillabubs, etc. Parmesan cheese, punch, wine, porter, beer.

A Girl's Life in Boston

The children of well-to-do parents often lived in a comfortable home with servants, but they also learned to work hard and to study. The following reading gives a glimpse into the life of twelve-year-old Anna Green Winslow. In 1770 Anna was sent from her home in Nova Scotia in Canada to live with her aunt and uncle in Boston so that she could go to school there.

In her letters to her mother, and occasionally to her father, Anna wrote lively reports describing her life and her progress in school. She was becoming increasingly interested in clothes, so she frequently wrote about her outfits in great detail.

⅍ ⅍ ⅍ ⅍ ⅍ ⅍ ⅍ ⅍ ⅍ ⅍ ⅍ ⅍ ⅍ ⅍ ⅍ ⅍

FROM

Anna Green Winslow's Diary

1772

Jany 17th, 1772

I told you the 27th **Ult** that I was going to a **constitution** with Miss Soley. I have now the pleasure to give you the result, viz. a very genteel well regulated assembly which we had at Mr Soley's last evening, Miss Soley being mistress of the ceremony. Mrs Soley desired me to assist Miss Hannah in making out a list of guests which I did some time since, I wrote all the invitation cards.

There was a large company assembled in a handsome, large, upper room in the new end of the house. We had two fiddles, & I had the honor to open the diversion of the evening in a minuet with miss Soley.

Our treat was nuts, raisins, Cakes, Wine, punch, hot & cold, all in great plenty. We had a very agreeable evening from 5 to 10 o'clock. For variety we **woo'd a widow, hunted the whistle, threaded the needle,** & while the company was collecting, we diverted ourselves with playing of **pawns.**

I was dress'd in my yellow coat, black bib & apron, black feathers on my head, my **paste**comb, & all my **paste** garnet, **marquheset** & **jet** pins, together with my silver plume—my loket, rings, black collar round my neck, black mitts & 2 or 3 yards of blue ribbin (black & blue is high tast), striped **tucker** and ruffles (not my best) & my silk shoes compleated my dress.

Feb 22d

I have spun 30 knots of **linning** yarn, and (partly) new footed a pair of stockings for Lucinda, read a part of the pilgrim's progress, coppied part of my text journal (that if I live a few years longer, I may be able to understand it, for aunt sais, that to her the contents as I first mark'd them, were an impenetrable secret). Play'd some, **tuck'd** a great deal (Aunt Deming says it is very true) laugh'd enough, & I tell aunt it is all human nature, if not human reason.

Ult: an abbreviation for the Latin word *ultimo,* meaning "last." So "27th Ult" means the twenty-seventh of last month.

constitution: an evening social.

woo'd a widow, hunted the whistle, threaded the needle, and ***pawns:*** popular games.

paste: glass made to look like gems used in jewelry and ornaments.

marquheset: a thin cotton or silk fabric on which to place pins.

jet: a form of coal used to create shiny, black jewelry.

tucker: a piece of linen or lace worn around the neck and shoulders.

linning: Anna's spelling of linen.

tuck'd: talked.

Pilgrim's Progress

John Bunyan's *Pilgrim's Progress*, published in the late 1600s, is a book of tales with moral themes, describing a pilgrim's travels through the "Celestial City." Bunyan's pilgrim was a pilgrim in the sense of a religious seeker, not one of the Pilgrim sect that arrived on the *Mayflower*. The book presented fundamental Puritan beliefs, and it remained popular through the 1800s. A number of Americans, including Abraham Lincoln, have considered it an important influence on their lives.

Benjamin Franklin: The First American

Benjamin Franklin returns to his brother James's printing shop for a visit after becoming a successful printer himself, April 1724.

Benjamin Franklin's life spanned most of the eighteenth century, from 1706 to 1790. From humble beginnings, he enjoyed great success as a businessman, printer and publisher, author, scientist, inventor, government official, philanthropist, and diplomat. His life and remarkable careers came to symbolize America as a land of opportunity. Among other achievements, Franklin helped make Philadelphia the first city to have a public library, a volunteer fire company, a paid police department, and street lighting. He also helped to establish the Pennsylvania Hospital and the school that became the University of Pennsylvania.

One reason that Franklin could pursue so many different interests was that he was very successful in his business as a printer. This selection from his *Autobiography* describes how he got his start in life.

✂ ✂ ✂ ✂ ✂ ✂ ✂ ✂ ✂ ✂ ✂ ✂ ✂ ✂ ✂ ✂

FROM

The Autobiography of Benjamin Franklin

1793

My elder brothers were all put **apprentices** to different trades. I was put to the grammar-school at eight years of age, my father intending to devote me, as the **tithe** of his sons, to the service of the Church. My early readiness in learning to read (which must have been very early, as I do not remember when I could not read), and the opinion of all his friends, that I should certainly make a good scholar, encouraged him in this purpose of his. . . . But, from the view of the expense of a college education . . . I was taken home to assist my father in his business, which was that of a **tallow-chandler** and **sope-boiler**. . . . Accordingly, I was employed in cutting wick for the candles, filling the dipping mold and the molds for cast candles, attending the shop, going of errands, etc.

I disliked the trade, and had a strong inclination for the sea, but my father declared against it; however, living near the water, I was much in and about it, learnt early to swim well, and to manage boats; and when in a boat or canoe with other boys, I was commonly allowed to govern, especially in any case of difficulty; and upon other occasions I was generally a leader among the boys, and sometimes led them into scrapes.

But my dislike to the trade continuing, my father was under apprehensions that if he did not find one for me more aggreeable, I should break away and get to sea, as his son Josiah had done, to his great vexation. He therefore sometimes took me to walk with him, and see joiners, bricklayers, turners, braziers, etc., at their work, that he might observe my inclination, and endeavor to fix it on some trade or other on land. It has ever since been a pleasure to me to

At age seventeen, Franklin ran away from his brother and made his way to Philadelphia. He arrived almost penniless, but found work with a printer and launched his career.

apprentice: a young person who learns a trade by working with a master of that craft.

tithe: a portion of one's assets or income given to the church.

tallow-chandler: someone who makes candles from *tallow* (beef fat).

sope-boiler: someone who makes soap.

Franklin's *Autobiography* wasn't published until 1793, after his death. The section reprinted here was probably written around 1771.

journeyman: when an apprentice was skilled enough, the master craftsperson considered him or her a journeyman— skilled at the craft but without his or her own shop.

see good workmen handle their tools; and it has been useful to me, having learnt so much by it as to be able to do little jobs myself in my house when a workman could not readily be got, and to construct little machines for my experiments, while the intention of making the experiment was fresh and warm in my mind.

From a child I was fond of reading, and all the little money that came into my hands was ever laid out in books. Pleased with the *Pilgrim's Progress*, my first collection was of John Bunyan's works in separate little volumes. . . . This bookish inclination at length determined my father to make me a printer, though he had already one son (James) of that profession. In 1717 my brother James returned from England with a press and letters to set up his business in Boston. I liked it much better than that of my father, but still had a hankering for the sea. To prevent the apprehended effect of such an inclination, my father was impatient to have me bound to my brother. I stood out some time, but at last was persuaded, and signed the indentures when I was yet but twelve years old. I was to serve as an apprentice till I was twenty-one years of age, only I was to be allowed **journeyman's** wages during the last year. In a little time I made great proficiency in the business, and became a useful hand to my brother.

Poor Richard's Almanac

One of Franklin's most popular achievements was his annual *Poor Richard's Almanac*. In addition to traditional almanac topics like the weather and farming, the sayings of Poor Richard became part of American folklore. Samples include "God heals, the doctor takes the fee" and "Keep thy shop, and thy shop will keep thee." New editions appeared every year from 1732 to 1757.

"*W*hat Then Is the American?"

By the mid-1700s the colonists knew they were creating a society far different from any in Europe. The countries of Europe had strict class lines, with royalty and nobles at the top, landless peasants and laborers at the bottom. In most of the countries as many as one-third of the people lived in poverty.

England was moving slowly toward democracy, but in the other European countries the people had little or no voice in government. In the colonies, however, the assemblies had a great deal of control over the affairs of each colony, and the people in the towns and villages were free to settle town matters.

Americans could easily see that their societies offered far greater freedom, self-government, and opportunity. One of the most famous statements about the American character and American society was written by an immigrant from France named J. Hector St. Jean de Crèvecoeur. This reading is called a letter, but it is really part of a series of essays he wrote on his farm in New York.

FROM

J. Hector St. Jean de Crèvecoeur's Letters from an American Farmer

C. 1782

A traveler to America is arrived on a new continent. A modern society offers itself, different from what he had previously seen. It is not composed, as in Europe, of great lords who possess everything, and of a herd of people who have nothing. Here are no noble families, no kings. The rich and the poor are not so far removed from each other as they are in Europe.

Some few towns excepted, we are all tillers of the earth. We are a people of farmers, scattered over a huge territory, united by a mild government. We all respect the laws,

Crèvecoeur went back to France in 1780, leaving his wife and two of his children on the farm. When he returned to New York in 1782, he found that Indians had killed his wife, destroyed his farm, and kidnapped his children. He recovered his children and, with their help, bravely started over. In spite of the personal tragedy, Crèvecoeur never lost his confidence in America and later published an expanded edition of *Letters*.

TO BE SEEN

Every Day, Sundays excepted,
At Trowbridge's Tavern,
in Green-Street, Albany

A BEAUTIFUL AFRICAN LION

This noble Animal is ten years old, three feet
four inches high, and measures eight feet from his
nosthrils, to the end of his tail; is of a beautiful dun
colour, and so gentle that he will lay down and rise
up at the command of his keeper. Those who have
seen the *LIONS* in the Tower of London, have re-
_____ the atten-

FRANCIS SYMONDS

At the Bell Inn, near Salem,

HEREBY informs the Public,

That he not only continueth to entertain *Gentlemen* and *Ladies* in the most agreeable manner, but
hath for S A L E, a good assortment of

ENGLISH AND WEST INDIA GOODS;

and that he not only grinds, but hath for Sale,
in large or small Quantities,

C H O C O L A T E

Which, he presumes to say, is as good and cheap
as any in the Government.

*If for Confirmation you incline,
And would have that that's genuine,
Then please to come and tr_____*

TO BE SOL_____

EIGHT GROCE OF EI_____
BUTONS, FOR HATTERS._____
Printer.

without dreading their power, because they are fair.
We are all moved with the spirit of hard work because
we work for ourselves.

If the visitor travels through our rural districts, he
views not the hostile castle contrasted with the clay-
built hut. The meanest of our log-houses is dry and
comfortable. Lawyer or merchant are the most noble
titles our towns offer. Farmer is the only title of the
rural inhabitants of our country.

There, on a Sunday, he sees at church respectable
farmers and their wives, all clad in neat homespun. We
have no princes for whom we toil, starve and bleed.
We are the most perfect society now existing in the
world. Here people are free as they ought to be. . . .

What then is the American, this new man? . . . He
is an American, who, leaving behind him all his
ancient prejudices and manners, receives new ones
from the new mode of life he has embraced, the new
government he obeys, and the new rank he holds. He
has become an American by being received in the
broad lap of our great Alma Mater. Here individuals
of all races are melted into a new race of man, whose
labors and posterity will one day cause great changes
in the world. Americans are
the western pilgrims.

SIR,

THE SMALL-POX STILL CONTINUES IN THE
FAMILIES of Mr. Hallowell, Dr. Clarke, and
Mr. Hodgson, as mention'd in your last paper, and
is not in any other Family in the Town.

Your humble Servant,
EZEKIEL GOLDTHWAIT, *Town-Clerk.*

THIS IS TO INFORM THE PUBLICK, that
the Small-Pox is broke out in the house of
Mr. Thomas Wood, a little below the Mills, on the
same side of the Way and in the house of Mr. Miller
on the Wharf near the Ferry (where Flags are hung
out according to Law) and in no other Place in the
Town.

BY ORDER OF THE SELECTMEN,
JOSEPH PHILLIPS, *Town Clerk.*

Charlestown, May 13, 1752.

B O U G H T   A N D
S O L D

ADVERTISEMENT

At the Barber Chyrurgeons Shop, joyning to the
Post-House, in Boston, is Bought all sorts of
Womens Hair, and Perriwiggs Made and Sold
Reasonably.

Very Good Candles, both for *Families* and *Ship-
ping*, to be sold very reasonably by ROBERT HEWES
at the Prison in *Queen Street*, Boston.

To be sold near OLIVER's BAKE-HOUSE, just by
the South Battery in Boston, a Number of very likely
NEGRO BOYS and GIRLS, just imported from Guinea.

*A selection of advertise-
ments and notices from
colonial newspapers.*

PART III

MANY PEOPLE, MANY VOICES

The thirteen English colonies grew rapidly in the 1700s. By the time of the American Revolution (1776–1783) the colonial population numbered more than two million people, who represented a mixture of nationalities and religions.

A little more than half the colonists traced their origins to England. Another large group, making up 20 percent of the population, were called the Scots-Irish. These were people whose ancestors were from Scotland and had settled for a time in Ireland. When they arrived in America, many of them followed the Appalachian Trail south, settling the "back country"—the western fringe of the southern colonies.

The rest of the white population were Dutch, French, Swedish, Danish, German, and a few other nationalities. These different groups were scattered among the colonies. The largest numbers settled in Pennsylvania. Other colonists called the Germans who settled in Pennsylvania the "Pennsylvania Dutch" because the name of their language—Deutsch—sounded like "Dutch."

Snakes for Prisoners

Ben Franklin became irritated at the large numbers of prisoners sent to America. The English, he said, were emptying their prisons and sending all the inmates to the colonies. Franklin's solution: Americans should send one rattlesnake to England for every prisoner sent to the colonies.

In the Middle Colonies and the South nearly half of all the immigrants during the 1700s were not entirely free—or were not free at all. Many white people came as indentured servants; others came as tenants of their European landlord or as apprentices bound to a master craftsperson. And more than 20,000 came as convicts, especially to Georgia. Most of the convicts were people who had been in prison in England because they could not pay their debts.

By far the largest numbers of the unfree immigrants were African slaves, dragged from their homelands and shipped to the New World in chains. It is estimated that between 500,000 and 600,000 people were brought to America in this way. By 1775 both slave and free people from Africa made up about one-fifth of the total population.

One other group, the Native Americans, was not counted in any of the official population figures. The Native American population east of the Appalachian Mountains declined rapidly in the 1700s. Some fled west to avoid the land rush of new settlers. Some were killed in wars. But the largest number died of diseases, such as smallpox, that had been brought by Europeans and against which their bodies had no defenses.

$\mathcal{S}$lavery on a Virginia Plantation

New slaves arrive on a Virginia plantation.

The first Africans were brought to America in 1619. Nineteen or twenty of them were sold in Virginia. The first Africans may have been treated as indentured servants and gained their freedom after a certain number of years. By the 1640s, however, laws had been passed making newcomers from Africa slaves for life. The number of slaves brought to the colonies in the 1600s remained small.

Around 1700 conditions in Europe and America led to a great increase in the number of slaves brought from Africa. In England and other parts of Europe a period of prosperity led to a reduction in the number of people wanting to

migrate to America as indentured servants. At the same time the plantations of the southern colonies were growing rapidly, creating a demand for slaves. Throughout the 1700s the number of slaves in the colonies increased steadily, especially in the South. By the time of the American Revolution, for example, the slave population of South Carolina was greater than the white population of that colony.

Philip Fithian was invited in 1773 to be a tutor at Nomini Hall, the manor house on the plantation of Colonel Robert Carter in Virginia. The plantation covered 600,000 acres, making it one of the largest in Virginia, and there were 600 slaves. In his diary Fithian described some of the surprises he experienced as he learned about life on a thriving plantation.

Household Expenses at Nomini Hall

Philip Fithian copied a ledger showing how much the household consumed in a year, including: 20 beef cattle, 350 bushels of wheat, 27,000 pounds of pork, 600 bushels of corn, 4 barrels of rum, and 150 gallons of brandy.

FROM
Philip Vickers Fithian's Journal
1773

Thursday, December 23, 1773. Except for some favorite slaves who wait on the table, their [the slaves'] weekly allowance is a **peck** of corn and a pound of meat apiece! And Mr. Carter is admitted by everyone to be, and from what I have already seen of others I have no doubt at all that he is, by far the most humane master to his slaves of any in this area! Good God! Are these Christians?

While I am on the subject, I will relate further what I heard Mr. George Lee's overseer Morgan say the other day that he had often done to Negroes himself and had found useful. He said that whipping of any kind does them no good, for they will laugh at your greatest severity. But he told us he had invented two things and proved their effectiveness by trying them several times. For sullenness, obstinacy, or laziness, he says, take a Negro, strip him, and tie him fast to a post. Then take a sharp **curry comb** and curry him severely until he is well scraped; then call a boy with some dry hay and make the boy rub him down for several minutes; and then salt him and release him. He will, said this human infidel, attend to his business afterwards!

peck: about eight quarts; the kernels of corn would first be cut off, then ground into meal to make cornbread. A pound of meat would make three or four servings.

curry comb: a brush with short wire bristles used for brushing horses.

A Traveler's View

Wealthy plantation owners in South Carolina spent the summer months in Charleston, where they maintained elegant homes cooled by ocean breezes. While they enjoyed weeks of social engagements, their foremen and slaves took care of crops on the inland plantations.

J. Hector St. Jean de Crevecoeur (see page 43) visited South Carolina sometime in the 1760s. He stayed at the homes of wealthy planters in Charleston and also visited plantations, including one managed by Eliza Lucas Pinckney (see page 34). The journey gave him another view of America.

FROM

J. Hector St. Jean de Crevecoeur's Letters from an American Farmer

c. 1782

While all is joy, festivity, & happiness in Charleston, would you imagine that scenes of misery overspread in the country? Their ears by habit are become deaf; their hearts are hardened . . . they do not see, hear, nor feel for the woes of their poor slaves from whose painful labors all their wealth proceeds. . . . The cracks of the whip urging these miserable beings to excessive labor are far too distant to be heard. . . .

With gold . . . they order vessels to the coasts of Guinea [West Africa]; by virtue of that gold, wars, murders, and devastations are committed in some harmless, peaceable African neighborhood where dwelt innocent people who even knew not but that all men were black. . . . Whole families swept away and brought through storms and tempests to this rich metropolis! There, arranged like horses at a fair, they are branded like cattle and then driven to toil, to starve, and to languish for a few years on the different plantations of these citizens.

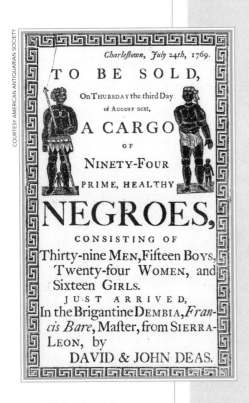

COURTESY AMERICAN ANTIQUARIAN SOCIETY

Broadside advertising a slave auction, 1769.

The Nightmare Atlantic Crossing

One of the most famous accounts of slave life in the 1700s was written by a former slave named Olaudah Equiano. Equiano was captured by slave traders in an African kingdom in northern Nigeria when he was eleven years old, but after about ten years of slavery in the West Indies, America, and on the high seas, he managed to purchase his freedom. His book, published in 1789, when he was forty-four, had the full title of *The Interesting Narrative of the Life of Olaudah Equiano or Gustavus Vassa the African,* but became more generally known as *Equiano's Travels.* It was sold widely in the new nation of the United States and helped make Americans aware of the evils of slavery. In the following reading he describes the Atlantic crossing experienced by all slaves who were captured in Africa and taken to North America.

Portrait of Olaudah Equiano, 1794.

F R O M

Equiano's Travels

1 7 8 9

The first object I saw when I arrived on the coast was the sea and a slave ship. The ship was riding at anchor and waiting for its cargo. These filled me with astonishment, which soon changed to terror. When I was carried on board I was handled by some of the crew to see if I were healthy. I now believed that I had got into a world of bad spirits. They were going to kill me.

I was not long allowed my grief . . . I was soon put down under the decks. There I received such an odor in my nostrils as I had never experienced before. So that with the disgusting smell and the crying I became so sick and low that I was not able to eat. When I refused food, I was beaten. . . .

The smell of the hold was so foul that it was dangerous to remain there for any time. The closeness of the place and the heat almost suffocated us. The ship was so crowded that we scarcely had room to turn. . . .

The groans of the dying made the whole a scene of horror almost not to be imagined. Because I was so young I was not put in chains.

The Middle Passage

The Atlantic crossing became known as the "Middle Passage" because it came between the ship's journey to Africa loaded with iron, cloth, brandy, and other goods to trade for slaves and the ship's trip from America back to Europe full of sugar, tobacco, and other products that the slave cargo had bought. Today the phrase "Middle Passage" is associated with all of the horrors of the slave's transatlantic experience.

Growing Opposition to Slavery

In the late 1760s some American colonists began to speak out against the British government's violation of their rights. This caused a number of people, including free blacks, to point out the contradiction of colonists demanding liberty while owning slaves. A group of free blacks in Boston petitioned the Massachusetts assembly to abolish slavery. In 1769 Thomas Jefferson, who himself owned slaves, was one of the first white Americans to suggest publicly that Virginia should consider a plan to pay slave owners for freeing their slaves. Jefferson's proposal was not considered seriously, and opposition to slavery remained weak throughout the colonial years. The following selection expresses the feeling of those who opposed slavery. An *epitaph* carved on a gravestone in Concord, Massachusetts, it describes the person buried there.

A Slave's Epitaph

1773

God
Wills us free
Man
Wills us slaves
I will as God wills,
God's will be done.

Here lies the body of JOHN JACK,
A native of Africa, who died in March, 1773,
Aged about sixty years.

Tho' born in a land of slavery,
He was born free.
Tho' he lived in a land of liberty,
He lived a slave.

Death, the grand Tyrant,
Gave him his final emancipation
And set him on a footing with kings.

Thomas Jefferson's Dilemma

In the 1770s Thomas Jefferson owned more than 100,000 acres of land in Virginia and nearly 200 slaves. Modern students of history are frequently troubled by the fact that Jefferson was both the author of the Declaration of Independence and the owner of slaves. Jefferson himself agonized over the issue of slavery throughout most of his life. These readings provide some evidence of his thinking over many years.

Mulatto: of mixed white and black ancestry.

corpulence: fat.

knavish: dishonest.

40 s., 4 l., and *10 l.:* 40 shillings, 4 pounds, and 10 pounds. Shillings and pounds were British monetary units.

Jefferson's Ad for the Return of a Runaway

1769

Run away from the subscriber in *Albemarle,* a **Mulatto** slave called *Sandy,* about 35 years of age, his stature is rather low, inclining to **corpulence,** and his complexion light; he is a shoemaker by trade, in which he uses his left hand principally, can do coarse carpenters work, and is something of a horse jockey; he is greatly addicted to drink, and when drunk is insolent and disorderly, in his conversation he swears much, and his behaviour is artful and **knavish.** He took with him a white horse, much scarred with traces, of which it is expected he will endeavour to dispose; he also carried his shoemakers tools, and will probably endeavour to get employment that way. Whoever conveys the said slave to me in *Albemarle,* shall have **40 s.** reward, if taken up within the county, **4 l.** if elsewhere within the colony, and **10 l.** if in any other colony, from

THOMAS JEFFERSON

FROM

Jefferson's Notes on the State of Virginia

1784

Indeed I tremble for my country when I reflect that God is just . . . a revolution of the wheel of fortune, an exchange of situation, is among possible events . . . I think a change already perceptible, since the . . . revolution. The spirit of the master is abating, that of the slave rising from the dust . . . the way I hope preparing, under the auspices of heaven, for a total **emancipation**.

FROM

Jefferson's Letter to Frances Epps

1787

I am miserable till I shall owe not a shilling; the moment that shall be the case I shall feel myself at liberty to do something for the comfort of my slaves.

I am decided against selling my lands. They are the only sure provision for my children. I have sold too much of them already. I am also unwilling to sell negroes, if the debt can be paid without. This unwillingness is for their sake, not my own; because my debts once cleared off, I shall try some plan of making their situation happier, determined to content myself with a small portion of their labor. I think it better for them therefore to be submitted to harder conditions for a while in order that they may afterwards be put into a better situation.

Nothing is more certainly written in the book of fate than that these people are to be free, nor is it less certain that the two races, equally free, cannot live in the same government.

—From Jefferson's *Autobiography*, 1819

First Encounters with Native Americans

One of the first Europeans to set foot in North America was John White, the great English watercolorist and governor of the ill-fated Roanoke colony (see page 4). In his journals he wrote and painted his impressions of Native American life.

FROM

John White's Journals

1585

John White's watercolor of the town of Secoton (now Beauford County, North Carolina).

Their towns that are not enclosed with poles are the handsomer ones, as shown by this drawing of the town of Secotan. For the houses are scattered here and there, and they have gardens in which they grow tobacco, called Uppowoc by the inhabitants. They also have forests in which they hunt deer and fields in which they plant their corn. In their corn fields, they build something like a scaffold on which they set a hut like a round chair where they station someone to watch, for there are so many birds and animals that unless they kept careful watch, they would soon devour all the corn. For this reason the watchman makes continual cries and noise. They plant their corn in a particular pattern; otherwise one stalk would choke the growth of another and the corn would not ripen. . . . They have also a separate broad area where they meet with their neighbors to celebrate their chief solemn feasts . . . and still another place where they make merry together after they have ended their feasts.

The Story of a "White Indian"

One useful source of information about the way of life of the many Native American tribes comes from whites who were captured by Indians and lived with them for a few weeks, months, or years—in some cases, many years. Some captives who were later returned to their people wrote of their experiences. These accounts vary widely. Some told of miserable lives of poverty; others suffered torture or mistreatment. And some wrote of kindness and a good life; in fact, many captives refused to go back to their natural families. These people were known as "White Indians."

The following reading is by an unusual White Indian named Mary Jemison. She was captured as a girl of about twelve during the French and Indian War (1756–1763) by Shawnee warriors and then was given to the Seneca. This selection from her book, printed in 1824, provides some insight into Indian ways of life, including the reason for taking captives.

William Penn's Experiences

In the 1680s William Penn visited many Indian villages in his new colony of Pennsylvania; he wanted to sign treaties of friendship with every tribe in the colony and to pay them for the land the settlers wanted. In a letter to friends in England in 1683, he described a visit to a Lenni-Lappee village. "If a European comes to . . . their House or Wigwam," Penn wrote, "they give him the best place. . . . If they come to visit us they salute with an Itah! which is as much as to say, 'Good be to you!' . . . If you give them anything to eat or drink . . . they are well pleased."

FROM

A Narrative of the Life of Mrs. Mary Jemison

1824

It is a custom of the Indians when one of their number is slain or taken prisoner in battle to give to the nearest relative . . . a prisoner if they have chanced to take one, and if not, to give him the scalp of an enemy. On the return of the Indians from conquest . . . the mourners come forward and make their claims. If they receive a prisoner, it is at their option either to **satiate** their vengeance by taking his life in the most cruel manner they can conceive of, or to receive and adopt him into the family in the place of him whom they have lost. . . .

satiate: satisfy.

squaw: a Native American woman.

Mary Jemison lived with the Indians until her death in 1833—at the age of ninety.

Indian Kidnappings

As Mary Jemison's story suggests, the taking of prisoners was quite common among the tribes—Indian prisoners as well as white—as a way of replacing members of the tribe. Estimates of the number of settlers taken prisoner vary widely. The practice continued when pioneers pushed westward and probably did not stop until the 1870s. It has been estimated that 10,000 white captives were taken before 1850.

It was my happy lot to be accepted for adoption, and at the time of the ceremony I was received by the two **squaws** to supply the place of their brother in the family, and I was ever considered and treated by them as a real sister, the same as though I had been born of their mother. . . .

Not long after the Delawares came to live with us at Wilshto, my sisters told me that I must go and live with one of them, whose name was Sheninjee. Not daring to cross them, or disobey their commands, with a great degree of reluctance I went, and Sheninjee and I were married according to Indian custom.

Sheninjee was a noble man: large in stature, elegant in his appearance, generous in his conduct, courageous in war, a friend to peace, and a great lover of justice. He supported a degree of dignity far above his rank, and merited and received the confidence and friendship of all the tribes with whom he was acquainted. Yet, Sheninjee was an Indian. The idea of spending my days with him at first seemed perfectly irreconcilable to my feelings, but his good nature, generosity, tenderness, and friendship towards me soon gained my affection, and, strange as it may seem, I loved him! To me he was ever kind in sickness and always treated me with gentleness; in fact, he was an agreeable husband and a comfortable companion. We lived happily together until the time of our final separation.

. . . Notwithstanding all that has been said against the Indians, in consequence of their cruelties to their enemies—cruelties that I have witnessed and had abundant proof of—it is a fact that they are naturally kind, tender and peaceable towards their friends, and strictly honest, and that those cruelties have been practiced only upon their enemies according to their idea of justice.

Mary Rowlandson

One of the most famous captives' stories—and one of the first—was the account written by Mary Rowlandson, captured during "King Philip's War" (1675–1676), when several tribes united to destroy many New England towns. Mrs. Rowlandson was captured by warriors of the Wampanoag tribe and taken to meet Metacomet (King Philip). During her eleven-week captivity she traveled, lived, and worked with the Wampanoag. She was finally ransomed, or bought back, for twenty pounds.

Mary Rowlandson's published account, in which she describes "the cruel and inhumane usage she underwent among the heathens," was hugely popular and helped to influence the way Americans and Europeans thought about the danger of living side by side with Native tribes.

Defending Diversity: Freedom of the Press and Speech

Many of America's most cherished freedoms and rights were ideals that emerged through the experiences of the colonial years. Religion offers a good illustration. When the Puritans arrived in the early 1600s, they wanted freedom to practice their own religion—but they did not want other religions in their colony. They established a government that supported the Puritan church.

As more and more religious groups emerged, the colonists had to change their thinking. They began by *tolerating*, or accepting, diversity of religious beliefs and then gradually extended that tolerance to a belief in freedom of religion. They also slowly began to separate the government from the church.

Another of America's most fundamental rights, *freedom of the press and speech*—the freedom of the people to write and say whatever they believed—also developed through colonial experiences. The single most important milestone in the development of this freedom was the trial of John Peter Zenger. Zenger, a German immigrant, was the publisher of one of the earliest newspapers in the colonies, the *New York Weekly Journal*.

Zenger's wife, Anna Catherine, continued to publish the *Journal* while he was in prison. They communicated through a hole in the door.

On an August morning in 1735, the courtroom in New York's City Hall was crowded with spectators for Zenger's trial. Zenger's crime? His newspaper had published articles that criticized the royal governor of New York, William Cosby. The governor clearly deserved to be criticized. He ruled the colony like a dictator, punishing any who opposed him and using bribery or threats to influence elections. But the people of New York had no public way to complain about Cosby—until Zenger began printing his four-page paper in 1733.

When an article attacked Cosby for influencing an election, he was furious. He ordered all copies of the *Journal* seized and publicly burned. Zenger was arrested and held in jail for eight months until the trial. The charge was seditious *libel*—statements criticizing an official in order to stir up rebellion.

The case hinged on the meaning of the word *libel*. The court said that, according to English law, any criticism of the government was libel. No one thought Zenger had a chance. The two attorneys assigned to defend Zenger were disbarred by the judges. But Zenger's defense was taken over by Andrew Hamilton of Philadelphia, a tall, white-haired man with a compelling voice, said to be the best attorney in the colonies. The following reading contains selections from Mr. Hamilton's concluding speech to the court. The jury found Zenger not guilty, and he was freed the next day.

COLLECTION OF THE NEW YORK HISTORICAL SOCIETY

Portrait of Alexander Hamilton.

The Trial as a Milestone

Hamilton's defense and Zenger's acquittal did not change the law, and the English government, through its royal governors, continued to interfere with what was published. Colonists never forgot the Zenger trial, however. Thirty years later they referred to the case, and to Hamilton's arguments, to justify their complaints against English rule.

FROM

Andrew Hamilton's Speech in the Trial of John Peter Zenger

1735

It is a right, which all free men claim, that they are entitled to complain when they are hurt. They have a right publicly to **remonstrate** against the abuses of power in the strongest terms, to put their neighbors upon their guard against the craft or open violence of men in authority, and to assert with courage the sense they have of the blessings of liberty, the value they put upon it, and their resolution . . . to preserve it as one of the greatest blessings heaven can bestow. . . .

. . . The man who loves his country prefers its liberty to all other considerations, well knowing that without liberty life is a misery. . . .

. . . The question before the Court and you, Gentlemen of the jury, is not of small or private concern. It is not the case of one poor printer, nor of New York alone . . . No! It may in its consequences affect every free man that lives in [British America]. It is the best cause. It is the cause of liberty . . . both of exposing and opposing arbitrary power . . . by speaking, and writing the truth.

Hamilton referred to freedom of speech as well as freedom of the press. Americans were beginning to see the two freedoms as inseparable—and that was how they were added to the Constitution.

remonstrate: to protest.

PART IV

PRELUDE TO REVOLUTION

In 1763 the British and the American colonists celebrated Great Britain's victory in a long war called the Seven Years' war. Indian tribes in the Ohio River Valley were angered that American colonists were crossing the Appalachians and moving into their lands. The tribespeople were supported by the French from their colony of Canada.

The war spread around the globe because Great Britain and France, the world's two most powerful nations, were in conflict in other parts of the world as well—in Europe, the Caribbean, and India and on the high seas. After several years of losses the British reversed the tide by focusing on North America, where they won overwhelming victories—with some help from the colonial militia.

The victory was a great one for the British. France gave up all land claims in North America, making Canada a huge new British colony. The American colonists shared in the pride of victory. Benjamin Franklin was asked whether, now that the French were gone, the colonies would think of uniting and seeking independence. Such a union, Franklin said, "is not merely improbable, it is impossible—I mean without the most grievous tyranny and oppression."

The readings in this part touch on the events that Americans saw as "the most grievous tyranny and oppression" and that led to the breakup of the union between Britain and its American colonies. Only twelve years after the victory celebrations in 1763 the colonists took up arms against the British to protect their rights. A year later the thirteen colonies declared their independence.

Patriots Protest a New Tax

Juggling Names

In 1707 the Kingdom of England and Wales was united with the Kingdom of Scotland to form the United Kingdom of Great Britain. From that time on the names England, Great Britain, or just Britain were all used interchangeably— although "Great Britain" was used most frequently.

Until 1765 the king and Parliament had ruled the colonies with a light touch, usually allowing them to run their own affairs. There were taxes— customs duties on goods coming into the colonies—but these were not very high, and the captain of a merchant ship might smuggle in a load of sugar now and then, or even give the customs collector a small bribe to avoid the customs duty.

But all that changed after the Seven Years' War. Great Britain was now the world's most powerful nation, with a huge empire to govern. The young King George III and his ministers in Parliament thought it only logical that the colonists should help pay the enormous cost of engaging in war and administering the empire.

In 1764 and 1765 the British Parliament passed a number of new laws. The customs regulations were tightened to stop smuggling, and smugglers were now to be tried in British courts rather than by a jury of their peers. The Quartering Act of March 1765 required colonial assemblies to find *quarters,* or barracks, for British soldiers, even in empty houses or other buildings.

All of these new measures irritated the colonists. They were strongly opposed to having British soldiers stationed in the colonies. But the measure that infuriated them the most was the Stamp Act of 1765. The act required that all paper used in the colonies have a special *seal,* or stamp, showing that a tax had been paid. The seal had to appear on everything from newspapers to birth certificates and marriage licenses to playing cards. While other acts annoyed the colonists, this one united them as well.

Anger over the Stamp Act spread rapidly from New Hampshire to Georgia. In every colony people who became known as *patriots* formed organizations called the Sons of Liberty and the Daughters of Liberty to start protests that might persuade Parliament and King George III to *repeal*, or remove, the hated tax. Patriotic merchants refused to trade with Great Britain. The Daughters of Liberty organized *boycotts*—asking all colonists to join them in refusing to buy any British goods. In the following selection, the newspaper publisher William Bradford explains to his readers that the Stamp Act is forcing him to suspend publication of his paper, the *Pennsylvania Journal*.

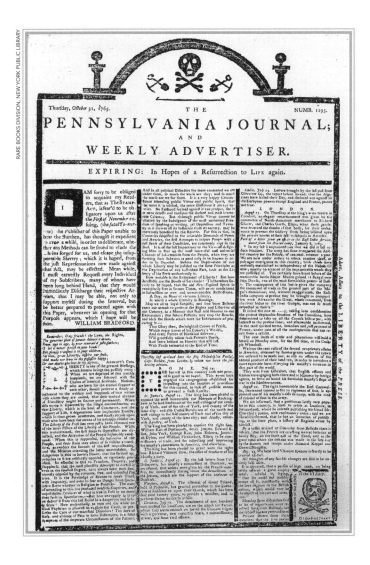

"No Taxation without Representation"

What upset the colonists most about the Stamp Act was that it was a direct tax—a tax levied directly on the people for the purpose of raising money. The colonists had no representatives in Parliament, so they had no voice in approving this new direct tax. The colonists accepted direct taxes from their colonial assemblies because they elected representatives to those assemblies. The argument was neatly summed up in a simple slogan: "No taxation without representation [in government]."

On October 31, 1765, newspaper publisher William Bradford printed the front page of his weekly newspaper to look like a tombstone. His message was clear: he could not afford to stay in business because of the excessive cost of the Stamp Act. In a corner of the page Bradford drew an "anti-stamp."

Documents requiring this stamp included insurance policies and probates of wills.

The real stamp.

The anti-stamp.

obligatory: required.

ensuing: coming up.

burthen: burden.

expedient: a good idea.

elude: avoid.

behind hand: owing money.

arrears: money owed.

FROM

The Pennsylvania Journal and Weekly Advertiser

OCTOBER 31, 1765

I am sorry to be obliged to acquaint my readers that as the Stamp Act is feared to be **obligatory** upon us after the *first of November* **ensuing** (The Fatal Tomorrow), the publisher of this paper, unable to bear the **Burthen,** has thought it **expedient** to stop a while, in order to deliberate, whether any methods can be found to **elude** the chains forged for us, and escape the insupportable slavery, which it is hoped, from the last representation now made against that act, may be effected. Mean while I must earnestly Request every individual of my Subscribers, many of whom have been long **behind Hand,** that they would immediately discharge their respective **Arrears,** that I may be able, not only to support myself during the Interval, but be better prepared to proceed again with this Paper whenever an opening for that purpose appears, which I hope will be soon.

WILLIAM BRADFORD

Community Spinning as Protest

The Daughters of Liberty managed to organize an almost complete boycott of British goods, especially clothing, cloth, and tea. They met in sewing bees and spinning bees to spin linen thread or wool yarn, then weave homespun garments. The first graduating class at Rhode Island College (later Brown University) even wore homespun to the graduation ceremony. The boycotts were so successful that British merchants petitioned Parliament to end the tax.

The Stamp Act Congress

In addition to the boycotts and protests organized by the Sons and Daughters of Liberty, the colonists also made a formal petition for a repeal of the Stamp Act. The Massachusetts assembly called for a meeting, or *congress,* of representatives of all the colonies to discuss some form of united protest. Nine colonies sent delegates to the Stamp Act Congress, which met in New York in October 1765.

The delegates were careful to express their loyalty to the king and Parliament; they were seeking to secure their rights as British subjects. Part of their declaration of their rights expressed that important new idea—that a government should be able to tax people only with the approval of their own elected representatives.

Stamp agent hanging in effigy—a figure or dummy representing an agent.

FROM

The Proceedings of the Congress

OCTOBER 1765

That His Majesty's liege subjects in these colonies are entitled to all the inherent rights and liberties of his natural-born subjects within the Kingdom of Great Britain.

That it is . . . essential to the freedom of a people, & the undoubted right of Englishmen, that no taxes be imposed on them without their own consent.

That the only representatives of the people of these colonies are persons chosen by themselves, and that no taxes ever have been or can be constitutionally imposed on them but by their respective legislature.

The delegates to the Stamp Act Congress, in addition to the declaration, sent petitions to King George III and to Parliament. All of their petitions were rejected.

The Beginning of a National Identity

The protests of the colonists, combined with the concern of British merchants about the business they were losing, led Parliament to repeal the Stamp Act early in 1766, but the patriots soon had more grievances. Parliament immediately passed what was called a Declaratory Act, stating that the British Parliament had the right to make laws for the colonies "in all cases whatsoever"—whether approved by the colonists' representatives or not. The colonists were also upset that British troops remained in America.

Parliament tried to impose other taxes, which were also met with protest, then repealed. By 1770 only a tax on tea remained. As the protests continued, many colonists were beginning to think of themselves in a new way—as a united people instead of just being residents of one colony or another. John Dickinson, a lawyer, farmer, and leading patriot, published his *Letters from a Pennsylvania Farmer* in 1767 and 1768. The letters became famous because of Dickinson's appeal for unity of all the colonies. In this selection, Dickinson protests the British suspension of the New York Assembly for failing to provide quarters to British troops.

Woodcut portrait of John Dickinson by Paul Revere, 1771.

RARE BOOKS DIVISION, NEW YORK PUBLIC LIBRARY

FROM

John Dickinson's Letters from a Pennsylvania Farmer

1 7 6 8

Whoever seriously considers the matter must perceive that a dreadful stroke is aimed at the liberty of these colonies. I say of these colonies; for the cause of one is the cause of all. If the Parliament may lawfully deprive New York of any of her rights, it may deprive any or all the other colonies of their rights; and nothing can possibly so much encourage such attempts as a mutual inattention to the interest of each other. To divide and thus to destroy is the first political maxim in attacking those who are powerful by their union. He certainly is not a wise man who folds his arms and reposes himself at home, seeing with unconcern the flames that have invaded his neighbor's house without using any endeavors to extinguish them. . . . When the slightest point touching the freedom of one colony is agitated, I earnestly wish that all the rest may with equal ardor support their sister. Very much may be said on this subject, but I hope more at present is unnecessary.

The Boston Massacre

The first real violence between the colonists and the British erupted in Boston on the night of March 5, 1770. An unorganized mob of men and boys was roaming the streets, taunting British soldiers on guard duty. The mood turned ugly. More soldiers arrived, including Captain Thomas Preston, who was in charge of the guards that night. In the confusion a shot was fired. More shots followed. After the violence was over three colonists lay dead, and two of those who were wounded had died by the next day.

This section includes a *broadside* written by Paul Revere. A broadside is a message or advertisement printed on a single sheet and circulated by hand or used like a poster to spread news. The broadside and the other readings illustrate a common problem in using firsthand accounts: when there are two or more versions of the same event, how can you tell which account is most accurate?

Patriots labeled the incident the "Boston Massacre" and used it to stir up anti-British feelings. The British, although they apologized for the deaths, treated the fatal encounter as a minor incident that was entirely the fault of the mob.

Portrait of Paul Revere by John S. Copley.

John Tudor was a church deacon who was sympathetic to the patriot cause but disliked mob action.

FROM

John Tudor's Diary

1770

On Monday evening the 5th, a few minutes after nine o'clock, a most horrid murder was committed in King Street before the customhouse door by eight or nine soldiers under the command of Captain Thomas Preston.

This unhappy affair began when some boys and young fellows threw snowballs at the sentry placed at the customhouse door. At this, eight or nine soldiers came to his aid. Soon after, a number of people collected. The Captain commanded the soldiers to fire, which they did, and three men were killed on the spot and several mortally wounded, one of which died the next morning.

FROM

Captain Thomas Preston's Letter to a Friend

1770

The British soldiers wore red coats, which led to such common nicknames as "redcoats," "lobsters," and "lobster backs."

The mob still increased and were more outrageous, striking their clubs . . . against another, and calling out, come on you rascals, you bloody backs, you lobster scoundrels, fire if you dare . . . we know you dare not. . . . At this time I was between the soldiers and the mob, [doing] all in my power to persuade them to retire peaceably, but to no purpose. They advanced to the points of the bayonets, struck some of them and even the muzzles of the pieces, and seemed to be [trying to start a fight] with the soldiers. . . . While I was thus speaking, one of the soldiers having received a severe blow with a stick, stepped a little on one side and instantly fired, on which . . . asking him why he fired without orders, I was struck with a club on my arm. . . . On this a general attack was made on the men by a great number of heavy clubs and snowballs being thrown at them . . . some persons at the same time from behind calling out . . . why don't you fire. Instantly three or four of the soldiers fired, one after another. . . . On my asking the soldiers why they fired without orders, they said they heard the word fire and supposed it came from me. This might be the case as many of the mob called out fire, fire, but I assured the men that I gave no such order; that my words were, don't fire, stop your firing.

Paul Revere was a well-known silversmith who played an important role in the American Revolution, especially in the early events leading to open warfare. Revere's propaganda broadsides, like the one on the Boston Massacre, helped to unify patriots throughout the colonies. His work as a courier—carrying information or news to patriot leaders throughout New England—was also important.

Trade card advertising Paul Revere and Son's Bell and Cannon Foundry, Boston, 1804.

Paul Revere's engraving of the Boston Massacre was widely printed throughout the colonies as a broadside.

Sam Adams: Spreading the Word

Sam Adams of Boston was one of the most active and radical of the patriots. He coined the term "Boston Massacre" and saw to it that Paul Revere's broadside was widely distributed.

Sam, whose cousin was the more sedate John Adams, always seemed to push the patriots in new directions. He started the idea of a "Liberty Tree" around which people would gather for protest rallies and meetings, and soon every town had one. On November 2, 1772, at his suggestion, the Boston town meeting appointed a "Committee of Correspondence . . . to state the rights of the Colonists and of this [Colony] in particular, as men, as Christians, and as subjects; and to communicate the same to the several towns and to the world." Soon every colony had a committee of correspondence. By sharing information in this way, the colonies were taking an important step toward unity.

The Boston Tea Party

In 1773 Parliament passed a new tea tax, ordering that all tea used in the colonies had to be purchased from England's East India Company. Once again the patriots were furious over a tax. It did not matter that tea—the favorite beverage in the colonies—would actually be cheaper; the patriots did not want the British interfering in their businesses.

The patriots in some seaport towns ordered the ships' captains to take the tea back to England; others allowed the tea to be unloaded and then locked it in warehouses. In Boston the Sons of Liberty dressed as Mohawk warriors, boarded the tea ships at dusk, and dumped all 342 chests of tea into Boston Harbor.

In the next selection, a young merchant named John Andrews describes the Boston Tea Party. The reading that follows describes John Adams's reactions.

FROM

A Letter by John Andrews

1773

They mustered, I'm told, on Fort Hill, about two hundred in number, and proceeded, two by two, to Griffins wharf . . . and before nine o'clock in the evening every chest on board the three vessels had been knocked to pieces and flung over the side. They say the participants were Indians from Narragansett. Whether they were or not, they appeared so to a casual observer, being clothed in blankets with their heads muffled, with copper colored faces, each being armed with a hatchet or axe and a pair of pistols. . . . Not the slightest insult was given to any person except a Captain Conner . . . who had ripped up the lining of his coat and vest under the arms and, watching for his opportunity, had nearly filled them with tea, but was detected and handled pretty roughly. They not only stripped him of his clothes but gave him a coat of mud, with a severe bruising in the bargain.

FROM

John Adams's Diary

1773

This is the most magnificent move of all. There is a dignity, a magesty, a sublimity in this last effort of the patriots that I greatly admire. The people should never rise without doing something to be remembered, something notable and striking. This destruction of the tea is so bold, so daring, so firm, intrepid and inflexible, that I can't help considering it a turning point in history. . . .

The question is whether the destruction of this tea was necessary? I think it was, absolutely and indispensably. They could not send it back. The Governor, Admiral and Comptroller would not permit it. It was in their power to save it, but in no one else's.

An artist's version of the Boston Tea Party.

"Give Me Liberty or Give Me Death"

The Boston Tea Party touched off a chain reaction that led directly to war—the American Revolution. News of the dumped tea infuriated King George III and his ministers. In the spring of 1774 Parliament passed a series of new laws, called the Coercive Acts, to punish Boston and the colony of Massachusetts. The port of Boston was closed until the patriots agreed to pay for the tea. Massachusetts lost most of its right to self-government. A military governor—General Thomas Gage—was placed in charge of the colony, and more British troops were sent to Boston.

People throughout the colonies were stunned by the laws, which they called the "Intolerable Acts." A continental congress was called to decide what to do. The First Continental Congress met in Philadelphia in September 1774, with fifty-six delegates from every colony except Georgia. The delegates passed a list of "resolves," demanding an end to the Coercive Acts, then passed a declaration of rights, including their right to decide tax matters. The Congress also set up a Colonial Association to enforce a boycott on all trade with Britain. Before adjourning in late October, the delegates agreed to meet again in May 1775.

Over the tense winter of 1774–1775, the towns of Massachusetts began preparing for war. They established special militia units—the *minutemen* who would be ready to "come in at a moment's notice."

In Virginia a meeting of the Virginia Convention was held in the spring of 1775. The representatives of the colony's assembly heard a powerful speech by Patrick Henry, a fiery patriot leader who had opposed the king's "tyranny" as early as 1763. His words became a rallying cry during the revolution.

FROM

Patrick Henry's Speech to the Virginia Assembly

1775

They tell us, sir, that we are weak; unable to cope with so **formidable** an **adversary.** But when shall we be stronger? Will it be the next week, or the next year?

. . . The battle, sir, is not to the strong alone; it is to the **vigilant,** the active, the brave. Besides, sir, we have no election [choice]. If we were base enough to desire it, it is now too late to retire from the contest. There is no retreat but in submission and slavery! Our chains are forged! Their

formidable: powerful or awe-inspiring.

adversary: opponent.

vigilant: watchful, alert.

Patrick Henry's speeches were famous for their power and eloquence, but they were not written down at the time. Fortunately, his friend and biographer, William Wirt, took careful notes and was able to reconstruct several of the most famous speeches. "Give Me Liberty" first appeared in print in Wirt's biography of Henry in 1817.

extenuate: to make something seem less serious.

clanking may be heard on the plains of Boston! The war is inevitable—and let it come! I repeat it, sir, let it come.

It is in vain, sir, to **extenuate** the matter. Gentlemen may cry, Peace, Peace—but there is no peace. The war is actually begun! The next gale that sweeps from the north will bring to our ears the clash of resounding arms! Our brethren are already in the field! Why stand we here idle? What is it that gentlemen wish? What would they have? Is life so dear, or peace so sweet, as to be purchased at the price of chains and slavery? Forbid it, Almighty God! I know not what course others may take; but as for me, give me liberty or give me death!

Patrick Henry delivering his great speech before the Virginia Assembly, March 23, 1775.

PART V

THE AMERICAN REVOLUTION

The winter of 1774–1775 was an uneasy time in British America. The British government insisted that the Boston patriots pay for the tea they had destroyed. The colonists had no intention of giving in.

In Boston General Thomas Gage was not sure what to do. He had a small army and a fleet of warships in the harbor, but he controlled only Boston. If he dared move inland, the colonial "minute-men" would swarm all over his troops.

The general's superiors, including young King George III, thought he was being wishy-washy, and they urged him to make a move. Gage didn't know how to tell them that there was a spy in Boston, probably on his staff, or maybe even in his household. Every time he planned a move, even when he sent a party to gather firewood, the patriots found out about it.

Finally Gage received an order he thought he could keep secret. He was to send a regiment of *British regulars* inland to the towns of Lexington and

Concord. Called "regulars" or "redcoats" for short—because of their red uniforms—these were British soldiers, as distinct from the German Hessians or the American loyalists who fought with the British. At Lexington they were to arrest two patriot leaders—Sam Adams and John Hancock—and at Concord they would seize a storehouse of weapons.

General Gage's order to send troops to Lexington and Concord led to the start of war between the colonies and Great Britain.

"One If by Land, Two If by Sea"

A spy in Boston sent word to a leading patriot, Dr. Joseph Warren, that General Gage was sending a column of troops (about one thousand men) to Lexington and Concord. Actually Gage sent only about 750 of the troops, holding the rest as a reserve under Lord Percy. Percy set off with this force at dawn, taking cannons with them, and helped the remainder of the redcoats get back to Charlestown and Boston. The spy did not know whether the troops would take boats across the bay to Charlestown or go the longer way by land across Boston Neck. Dr. Warren alerted the patriots' best courier, Paul Revere, to warn John Hancock and Sam Adams—and the minutemen of all the towns around Lexington and Concord—of the troops' approach.

Revere asked a friend to wait in the tower of the Old North Church with two lanterns. If the regulars marched by the land route, he was to show one lantern from the bell tower; if they took boats across the bay, he was to show two lanterns—"One if by land, two if by sea."

Revere, meantime, rowed across the bay to Charlestown where friends were waiting for him. The signal had already appeared—two lanterns—but Revere now had a good head start. He knew that Dr. Warren had also sent another messenger, John Dawes, by the land route earlier. Here is part of Revere's account from a long letter he wrote in 1798 to Dr. Jeremy Belknap, one of America's earliest historians.

The Fame of Paul Revere

Paul Revere was a well-known patriot, but his ride was hardly remembered in the years after the Revolution. That is, until some eighty years later, when the American poet Henry Wadsworth Longfellow wrote his famous poem "The Midnight Ride of Paul Revere."

FROM

Paul Revere's Letter to Dr. Jeremy Belknap

1798

I set off upon a very good horse; it was then about eleven o'clock and very pleasant. After I had passed Charlestown Neck, I saw two men on horseback under a tree. When I got near them, I discovered they were British officers. One tried to get ahead of me, and the other to take me. I turned my horse very quick and galloped towards Charlestown Neck, and then pushed for the Medford Road. The one who chased me, endeavoring to cut me off, got into a clay pond near where Mr. Russell's Tavern is now built. I got clear of him, and went through Medford, over the bridge and up to Menotomy. In Medford, I awaked the captain of the minute men; and after that, I alarmed almost every house, till I got to Lexington.

Revere's Alarm

As Revere rode through the sleeping villages west of Boston, he would not have shouted, "The British are coming!" The word *British* applied to civilians, not just soldiers. And at the time the colonists still thought of themselves as British citizens. We know from Revere's own account that what he actually said was, "The regulars are coming!" There would have been no mistake about who the regulars were.

Who Was the Patriot Spy?

General Gage had tried hard to keep the march to Lexington and Concord a secret. The soldiers were not told until it was time to march. One of the regulars wrote: "The men marched through the streets [of Boston] with the utmost silence. . . . A dog, happening to bark, was instantly killed with a bayonet."

While the British were tiptoeing to their boats, Revere and Dawes were already on their way. The speed with which this secret got out convinced Gage that the spy was in his own household, and he must have suspected his wife. After all, she came from a leading patriot family in New York—the Schuylers. Gage was recalled to London a few weeks later, and the couple separated soon after their arrival. Was she the spy? Was this the reason for their separation? No direct evidence of her guilt has been found, but many historians have concluded that she was the one whose word sent Revere on his midnight ride.

The Battle of Lexington

The 750 British troops sent to Lexington and Concord left Boston just before midnight on April 18, 1775. Dawn was just breaking when they approached the village of Lexington, a distance of about twelve miles.

The alarm spread by Paul Revere, John Dawes, and others had awakened every village for miles around. In this first reading, one of the minutemen, Ebenezer Munroe, describes the opening encounter between the minutemen and the British regulars, or redcoats, at Lexington.

FROM

Ebenezer Munroe's Diary

1775

The last person sent [toward Cambridge] was Thaddeus Bowman, who returned between daylight and sunrise and informed Capt. Parker that the British troops were within a mile of the meeting-house. Capt. Parker immediately ordered the drum beat to arms. I was the first that followed the drum. I took my station on the right of our line, which was formed from six to ten **rods** back of the meeting-house, facing south.

About seventy of our company had assembled when the British troops appeared. . . . Some of our men went into the meeting-house, where the town's powder was kept. . . . When the regulars had arrived within eighty or one hundred rods, they, hearing our drum beat, halted, charged their guns, and doubled their ranks, and marched up at quick step. Capt. Parker ordered his men to stand their ground, and not molest the regulars unless they meddled with us. The British troops came up directly in our front. The commanding officer advanced within a few rods of us and exclaimed, "Disperse, you damned rebels! You dogs, run!— Rush on, my boys!" and fired his pistol.

The British insisted that it was the rebels, not the British, who fired the first shots.

rod: a unit of distance equal to about five and a half yards.

THE CONNECTICUT HISTORICAL SOCIETY, HARTFORD, CONNECTICUT

A depiction of the Battle of Lexington by Amos Doolittle, a silversmith from New Haven, Connecticut, who visited the area soon after the battle and interviewed participants for his painting.

Battle Nerves

The minutemen were special units of each town's militia. They had received extra training over the winter of 1774–1775 and all were ready to answer an alarm at a moment's notice. A young corporal, John Munroe, described how the excitement affected his loading of his musket: "After I had fired the first time, I retreated about ten rods, and then loaded my gun a second time, with two balls, and, on firing at the British, the strength of the charge took off about a foot of my gun barrel."

The Battle of Concord

The brief Battle of Lexington left eight patriots dead and about ten wounded; one British soldier received a mild leg wound. The British then marched on to Concord, where they expected to find a store of weapons. But the patriots had had enough warning to hide most of the supplies.

In Concord the British force divided into three groups—one to occupy the village, a second to guard a bridge (Concord's "Old North Bridge"), and the third went to search a farm where spies had reported the weapons would be located.

The minutemen, outnumbered as the British approached, retreated through the village, crossed the bridge, and took up positions behind stone walls.

Minuteman Thomas Thorp described the scene as he arrived.

ball: ammunition for a musket.

fifer: the player of a fife (an instrument like a flute).

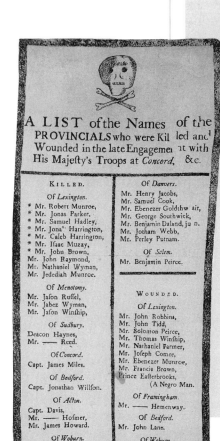

A list of the names of the patriots killed or wounded in the Battle of Concord.

FROM

Thomas Thorp's Journal

1775

We found a great collection of armed men, from Concord and other towns. There were several hundreds, cannot say how many. . . . Our officers joined the others. Three companies of redcoats was on the other side of the north bridge and a few begun ripping up planks from the bridge. . . .

At the same time, several Concord men shouted "Smoke! The redcoats are torching our town . . ." Captain [Isaac] Davis returned to [us] and drew his sword, and said to the company, "I haven't a man that is afraid to go," and gave the word "March!"

The redcoats run from the bridge and others shot toward us, dropping shots meant to warn and I saw where a **ball** threw up the water about the middle of the river.

Their next shots was to kill for I heard our young **fifer** cry out he had been hit, and a major near me shouted "Fire, fellow soldiers! For God's sake, fire."

"The Shot Heard 'Round the World"

Although the first shots had been fired earlier at Lexington, Ralph Waldo Emerson chose the encounter at the North Bridge to immortalize as "the shot heard 'round the world" in his poem "Concord Hymn." Emerson's father, Reverend William Emerson, watched the battle from his house, located about one hundred yards from the bridge.

Music for Marching, Music for Fighting

Every military company had drummers and fifers who played steadily during marches to keep the men moving in unison and to keep their spirits high for battle. The musicians were often young boys. A young Concord minuteman, Corporal Amos Barrett, reported on the minutemen's march out to meet the redcoats, who were coming toward them from Lexington: "[The British] got within about 100 rods of us, then we were ordered to the about face and now marched before them with our drums and fifes agoing, and the British the same. We had grand music."

When the minutemen advanced on Concord's North Bridge, the patriot fifes and drums played a lively tune called "The White Cockade." And when Lord Percy's relief column approached Lexington, the British defiantly played "Yankee Doodle"—a patriot song.

*W*ashington Takes Charge

Events moved swiftly after the Battles of Lexington and Concord. The militia from all the towns around Boston did not go home after those historic first shots. Instead, they established crude camps outside the city and waited to see what the British planned to do. The British were essentially trapped in Boston, facing the campfires of fifteen thousand or more patriot militia.

The Second Continental Congress convened on May 10, 1775. The representatives of the Congress, which was now functioning as the government of the colonies, agreed that the best of the militia should be formed into a Continental Army. To organize and command the army, they chose George Washington of Virginia.

As a twenty-one-year-old colonel in 1755, Washington had gained a reputation for bravery in the French and Indian War. In 1775 he was a member of the Congress, a wealthy plantation owner, and an imposing figure at six-foot-three and two hundred pounds. Beside his military record, John Adams also nominated Washington because he was a

Virginian. The British and all Americans would see that colonies outside Massachusetts were committed to the cause.

General Washington arrived in Cambridge, outside Boston, early in July 1775 and began organizing an army. While the patriots were determined to carry on this war to protect their liberties, only a few radicals were yet thinking of independence. They still thought of themselves as British citizens. Washington, for example, at every evening meal with his staff officers, always proposed a toast to the health of King George III.

In the next reading, first impressions of Washington are given by Dr. James Thacher, a young physician who stayed with the Continental Army throughout the long conflict and kept one of the most detailed and insightful diaries of the American Revolution. That selection is followed by one in which Washington expresses his uneasiness about the task he has taken on.

The uniform was Washington's own design, and the blue and buff became standard for the Continental Army.

FROM

The Military Journal of Dr. James Thacher

1775

I have been much gratified this day with a view of General Washington. His excellency was on horseback, in company with several military gentlemen. It was not difficult to distinguish him from all others. His personal appearance is truly noble and majestic, being tall and well proportioned. His dress is a blue coat with **buff**-colored facings, a rich epaulette on each shoulder, buff under-dress, and an elegant small sword; a black cockade in his hat.

buff: the color of sand.

FROM

George Washington's Letter to Martha Washington (Patsy)

1775

You may believe me, my dear Patsy, when I assure you in the most solemn manner that, so far from seeking this appointment, I have used every endeavour in my power to avoid it . . . not only from my unwillingness to part with you and the family, but from a consciousness of its being a more real happiness in one month with you at home than I have the most distant prospect of finding [away], if my stay were to be seven times seven years.

But as it has been a kind of destiny that has thrown me upon this service, I shall hope that my undertaking it is designed to answer some good purpose.

The Battle of Bunker Hill

While the Congress considered Washington's appointment, the patriots outside Boston had fought another stirring battle against the redcoats—the Battle of Bunker Hill (actually fought on Breed's Hill) on June 17, 1775. The patriots had fortified the hill at night and the British attacked it the next day. The patriots put up a spirited defense, turning back two charges before running out of ammunition and yielding the hill on the third attack. Out of 2,250 British in the battle, nearly half—1,054—were killed or wounded, including 92 officers. The American losses were 140 killed, 271 wounded. Although the patriots technically lost the battle, they were encouraged that their untrained army of farmers and seamen had stood up so well to a professional army.

Letter from a Patriot

Once the war had begun, every colonist had to decide how he or she would respond. Nearly one-third of the people remained loyal to Britain and became known as *loyalists*. A slightly larger number were patriots. But about another one-third were either indifferent or shifted position, depending on which side seemed to be winning or could offer the most incentives.

People frequently debated the issue with friends or family members, and some families became hopelessly divided. Ben Franklin, for example, was a leading patriot, but his son, William Franklin, governor of New Jersey, remained an ardent loyalist. In the following letter, a Philadelphia woman, Elizabeth Bartlett, explained her beliefs to a friend, a British officer stationed in Boston. The exact date of the letter is not known.

FROM

Elizabeth Bartlett's Letter to a British Officer

I will tell you what I have done. My only brother I have sent to the camp with my prayers and my blessings. I hope he will not disgrace me. I am confident he will behave with honor.

Had I twenty sons and brothers they should go. I have cut back every unnecessary expense in my family. Tea I have not drunk since last Christmas. Nor have I bought a new cap or gown. Although I have never done it before, I have learned to knit. I am now making stockings of American wool. This way I do my bit for the public good.

I know this—that as free I can die but once. But as a slave I shall not be worthy of life.

I have the pleasure to assure you that these are the feelings of all my sister Americans. Our husbands, brothers, and sons are as with one heart determined to die or be free. It is not a trifle that we are fighting for. It is this plain truth—that no one has a right to take their money without their consent.

You say you are no politician. Oh, sir, it requires no

scheming head to discover this tyranny and oppression. It is written with a sunbeam. Everyone shall see and know it. And we shall be unworthy of the blessings of Heaven if we ever submit to it.

A Patriot Marching Song

If Americans had a favorite marching song it had to be "Yankee Doodle." The British had their own versions (and the tune itself is English), which they used to poke fun at the Americans. The term *Yankee* was a derogatory (insulting) label for a New Englander, and *Doodle* meant a dolt or a fool. Nonetheless, Americans themselves were even fonder of the song than the British, and they created almost endless variations. Just as Americans liked to be called "rebels," they seemed to take pride in "Yankee Doodle." The refrain followed each verse.

FROM

"Yankee Doodle"

Father and I went down to camp
Along with Captain Gooding,
And there we saw the men and boys
As thick as hasty pudding.

(Refrain) Yankee Doodle keep it up,
Yankee Doodle Dandy,
Mind the music and the step,
And with the girls be handy.

There was Captain Washington
Upon a slapping stallion
A-giving orders to his men—
There must have been a million.

The verse of "Yankee Doodle" best known to present-day Americans was not part of the version reprinted here.

Yankee Doodle went to town
Riding on a pony,
He stuck a feather in his cap
And called it macaroni.

Engraved for BARNARD's New Complete & Authentic HISTORY of ENGLAND.

Portrait & Uniform of An
AMERICAN GENERAL.

A real representation of the Dress of An
AMERICAN RIFLE-MAN.

*The uniforms of an
American general and
a rifleman.*

Deborah Champion's Ride

Many women and girls acted bravely, even heroically, during the Revolutionary War. One example is the daring ride of a young woman named Deborah Champion, who was asked by her father, General Henry Champion, to take some important papers from their home in Connecticut to Washington's headquarters outside Boston. In a letter to a friend, Deborah, who was about twenty years old, described her mission.

FROM
Deborah Champion's Letter to a Friend
1775

My Dear Patience:

I would have answered your last letter long before now, but I have been away from home. I know that you will hardly believe that such a stay-at-home as I should go and all alone too, to where do you think? To Boston! I will tell you all about it. . . .

So, dear Patience, it was finally settled that I should start in the early morning. Before it was fairly light, mother called me, though I had seemed to have hardly slept at all. I found a nice hot breakfast ready, and a pair of saddle-bags packed with such things as mother thought might be needed. Father told me again of the haste with which I must ride and the care to use for the safety of the messages.

The British were at Providence, in Rhode Island, so it was thought best I should ride due north to the Massachusetts line, and then east to Boston. Hiding my papers in a small pocket in the saddle-bags under all the eatables mother had filled them with, I rode on. I was determined to ride all night. It was very early in the morning that I heard the call of the sentry. Now, if at all, the danger point was reached.

Pulling my bonnet still farther over my face, I went on. Suddenly, I was ordered to halt. I did so. A soldier in a red coat proceeded to take me to headquarters. I told him it was too early to wake the captain, and to please let me pass. I said I had been sent in haste to see a friend in need. That was true, if misleading. To my joy, he let me go. Evidently he was as glad to get rid of me as I of him.

That is the only bit of adventure that befell me in the whole long ride. When I arrived in Boston, I was so very fortunate as to find friends who took me at once to General

Symbols of Unity

In 1775, when many patriots were promoting a sense of unity among the colonies, they turned to a symbol of that unity that had first been drawn by Benjamin Franklin in 1754. In a political cartoon Franklin showed the thirteen colonies as parts of a snake. His point was simple: the colonies had to work together or they would not survive. The initials in the cartoon stand for the names of nine colonies, plus New England, which included Connecticut, Massachusetts, Rhode Island, and New Hampshire. (Maine and Vermont were not yet states.)

The famous "Unite or Die" symbol.

Washington. I gave him the papers, which proved to be of great importance.

He complimented me most highly on the courage I had displayed and my patriotism. Oh, Patience, what a man he is, so grand, so kind, so noble. I am sure we will not look to him in vain to save our fair country for us.

Women Couriers

A number of young patriot women made daring rides carrying important messages, often going through enemy lines. When a British war party landed on the Connecticut coast in 1777, for example, sixteen-year-old Sybil Ludington rode forty miles through a moonless night to alert the militia.

Some other heroic rides: late in the war, in 1781, Emily Geiger rode one hundred miles through South Carolina carrying messages to General Nathaniel Greene of the Continental Army; in the same year, teenager Susanna Bolling crossed the Appomattox River to warn Americans of an approaching British force; and Betsy Dowd, another sixteen-year-old, warned Virginia militia of a planned invasion at Norfolk.

A Black Poet Writes of Freedom

In 1761 a young black girl was brought to America as a slave and purchased by John Wheatley, a Boston tailor. The Wheatleys gave her the first name Phillis and their last name. They educated her, encouraged her talent as a poet, and eventually gave her her freedom. By 1770 her religious and political poems were being published in newspapers, and a book of her poetry made her famous. In the poem included here, addressed to the British Secretary of State for North America, the Earl of Dartmouth, she explains that her love of freedom came from losing her freedom when she was seized by slavers; the poem suggests that Britain's tyranny over the colonists has made them lovers of freedom.

FROM
Phillis Wheatley's "To the Earl of Dartmouth . . ."
1773

Should you, my lord, while you peruse my song,
Wonder from whence my love of Freedom sprung,
Whence flow these wishes for the common good,
By feeling hearts alone best understood,
I, young in life, by seeming cruel fate
Was snatch'd from Afric's fancy'd happy seat:
What pangs excruciating must molest,
What sorrows labour in my parent's breast?
Steel'd was the soul and by no misery mov'd
That from a father seiz'd his babe belov'd:
Such, such my case. And can I then but pray
Others may never feel tyrannic sway?

Portrait of the American poet Phillis Wheatley.

George and Phillis

While General Washington was directing the placement of cannons outside Boston, he took the time to write to Phillis Wheatley, thanking her for a poem she had written about him.

"If you should ever come to Cambridge, or near headquarters, I shall be happy to see a person so favored by the muses & in whom nature has been so liberal & beneficent in her dispensations." Apparently the two did meet in 1775 or early 1776, but there is no record of what they said.

Declaring Independence

By the end of 1775 Americans had been fighting the British since the previous April. But even though many had already sacrificed their lives for America's liberty, most people were not yet ready to break completely with Great Britain by declaring independence.

Two events helped to change public opinion. First, in December 1775, Parliament passed the Prohibitory Acts, declaring that a state of war existed with the colonies (and prohibiting trade with them). The Parliament and King George were giving the Americans the status of a foreign nation. To many patriots, this declaration was like saying that the colonies were, in fact, already independent.

The second event was the publication of a pamphlet called *Common Sense* in January 1776—one of the most famous and influential publications in America's history. In only a few months an amazing 150,000 copies were in circulation. Although no author was listed on the pamphlet, people soon learned that it had been written by Thomas Paine, a recent immigrant from England, who became a leading patriot writer.

The following reading contains some of the important passages in *Common Sense*. Note that Paine usually refers to America as "the continent."

FROM

Thomas Paine's Common Sense

1 7 7 6

In the following pages I offer nothing more than simple facts, plain arguments, and common sense. . . .

Volumes have been written on the subject of the struggle between England and America. Men of all ranks have embarked on the controversy . . . but all have been **ineffectual**, and the period of debate is closed. Arms as a last resource will decide the contest; the appeal [to arms] was the choice of the king, and the continent has accepted the challenge.

ineffectual: powerless, useless.

Everything that is right or natural pleads for separation [from England]. The blood of the slain, the weeping voice of nature cries, TIS TIME TO PART. Even the distance at which the Almighty hath placed England and America is a strong and natural proof that the authority of the one over the other, was never the design of Heaven. . . .

. . . Small islands not capable of protecting themselves are the proper objects for kingdoms to take under their care; but there is something very absurd in supposing a continent to be perpetually governed by an island.

. . . Independency means no more than this: whether we shall make our own laws, or whether the king, the greatest enemy which this country hath, shall tell us, *There shall be no laws but such as I like.* . . .

O ye that love mankind! Ye that dare oppose not only the tyranny but the tyrant, stand forth! Every spot of the old world is overrun with oppression. Freedom hath been hunted round the globe. Asia and Africa have long expelled her. Europe regards her like a stranger, and England hath given her warning to depart. O receive the fugitive, and prepare in time an **asylum** for mankind.

PRINTS COLLECTION, NEW YORK PUBLIC LIBRARY

Engraving of Thomas Paine by W. Sharp, 1793.

asylum: a safe place.

The British Evacuate Boston

When the war began at Lexington and Concord in the spring of 1775, two ambitious patriots—Benedict Arnold and Ethan Allen—led an attack on Fort Ticonderoga near the southern tip of Lake Champlain in New York. They easily captured the fort and about seventy valuable cannons. Over the winter of 1775–1776 the cannons captured at Fort Ticonderoga were hauled more than 150 miles to Washington's troops outside Boston. The task of moving the cannons was given to General Henry Knox, a rather portly Boston book dealer who had read

many books about cannons and later was placed in command of the Continental Army's artillery.

Early in the spring of 1776 the cannons were placed on the heights overlooking Boston. When the British in Boston saw the cannons, they were convinced that they could not hold on in Boston any longer. Through an exchange of messages, Washington agreed not to fire on the evacuation; in exchange, General William Howe agreed not to burn the city.

There was great rejoicing as the British boarded their ships and set sail for Canada. Ten years later the Continental Congress had a medal struck to honor General Washington and the evacuation.

Cannons being hauled from Fort Ticonderoga across the rugged mountains of western Massachusetts to Boston, by the artist Tom Lovell.

Thirteen United States Declare Independence

By May 1776 the members of the Congress were ready to consider the great issue of declaring independence. A committee of five was named to prepare a draft. The committee chose Thomas Jefferson to write the draft, and John Adams and Benjamin Franklin to review it and make changes. Robert Livingston and Roger Sherman were the other two committee members.

The draft was submitted to the Congress on July 2. After some debate, the Congress approved the Declaration of Independence on July 4. The delegation from Delaware was evenly divided, so delegate Caesar Rodney rode all night through a fierce thunderstorm to break the tie. All the colonies voted in favor, except New York, which abstained.

The Declaration is divided into three sections: In the first section, Jefferson explains what is called the *compact,* or contract, theory of government—that government is a contract between the government and the people. If the government fails to protect people's natural rights, they can overthrow that government and create a new one. In the second section (not included here), the document spells out the abuses of King George III. The third section states that, having tried and failed to have the wrongs corrected, the representatives of the people now declare their independence from Great Britain.

FROM

The Declaration of Independence

1776

When in the Course of human events, it becomes necessary for one people to dissolve the political bands which have connected them with another, and to assume among the powers of the earth, the separate and equal station to which the Laws of Nature and of Nature's God entitle them, a decent respect to the opinions of mankind requires that they should declare the causes which impel them to the separation.

We hold these truths to be self-evident, that all men are created equal, that they are endowed by their Creator with certain **unalienable** Rights, that among these are Life, Liberty and the pursuit of Happiness.—That to secure these rights, Governments are instituted among Men, deriving their just powers from the consent of the governed,—That whenever any Form of Government becomes destructive of these ends, it is the Right of the People to alter or to abolish it, and to institute new Government, laying its foundation on such principles and organizing its powers in such form, as to them shall seem most likely to effect their Safety and Happiness. Prudence, indeed, will dictate that Governments

unalienable: not to be separated or taken away.

sufferable: tolerable; capable of being endured.

usurpations: the illegal exercise of authority or privilege; taking something by force or without right.

evinces: shows.

despotism: rule by absolute authority; tyranny.

sufferance: the capacity to tolerate pain or distress; endurance.

Supreme Judge: God.

rectitude: moral uprightness.

absolved: to pronounce clear of blame or guilt; released from obligation.

Submitting the Declaration of Independence to Congress, July 2, 1776.

long established should not be changed for light and transient causes; and accordingly all experience hath shewn, that mankind are more disposed to suffer, while evils are **sufferable,** than to right themselves by abolishing the forms to which they are accustomed. But when a long train of abuses and **usurpations,** pursuing invariably the same Object **evinces** a design to reduce them under absolute **Despotism,** it is their right, it is their duty, to throw off such Government, and to provide new Guards for their future security.—Such has been the patient **sufferance** of these Colonies; and such is now the necessity which constrains them to alter their former Systems of Government. The history of the present King of Great Britain is a history of repeated injuries and usurpations, all having in direct object the establishment of an absolute Tyranny over these States. . . .

In every stage of these Oppressions We have Petitioned for Redress in the most humble terms: Our repeated Petitions have been answered only by repeated injury. A Prince whose character is thus marked by every act which may define a Tyrant, is unfit to be the ruler of a free people.

We, therefore, the Representatives of the united States of America, in General Congress, Assembled, appealing to the **Supreme Judge** of the world for the **rectitude** of our intentions, do, in the Name, and by Authority of the good People of these Colonies, solemnly publish and declare, That these United Colonies are, and of Right ought to be Free and Independent States; that they are **Absolved** from all Allegiance to the British Crown, and that all political connection between them and the State of Great Britain, is and ought to be totally dissolved; and that as Free and Independent States, they have full Power to **levy** War, conclude Peace, contract Alliances, establish Commerce, and to do all other Acts and Things which Independent States may of right do.

And for the support of this Declaration, with a firm reliance on the protection of **divine Providence,** we mutually pledge to each other our Lives, our Fortunes and our sacred Honor.

levy: to carry on.

divine Providence: the care, guardianship, and protection of God.

Signing and Distributing the Document

On July 4, 1776, only two men signed the Declaration of Independence: John Hancock, president of the Congress, and Charles Thomson, the secretary. Three days were then needed to make copies of the Declaration; the first public reading in Philadelphia did not take place until July 8. In New York the Declaration was read to Washington's troops the following day. Most of the fifty-six signers added their names on August 2.

A facsimile of the Declaration of Independence.

"We Must All Hang Together. . ."

The signers of the Declaration of Independence were keenly aware that, in British eyes, they were guilty of treason. This is one of the reasons Congress debated the issue so long, even though the people had been ready for a Declaration for several months. After signing the document, Benjamin Franklin said, "Now we must all hang together, or most assuredly

The Dangers the Signers Faced

After most of the fifty-six signers had added their signatures to the Declaration of Independence, their names were kept secret for several months to protect them from the anger of the British or the loyalists. When the British took control of a region or a city—New York, Philadelphia, and Charleston were all occupied at some time—they made life very hard on any signers they found. Many saw all of their property destroyed and lost their fortunes. Some were also imprisoned.

solicitude: anxiety.

subscribed: signed.

pensive: thoughtful.

pervaded: spread throughout.

solemnity: seriousness.

we will all hang separately." In a letter to John Adams, Dr. Benjamin Rush, who also signed the Declaration, recalls the anxiety that the signers lived with until the Americans won the Revolution. Like Franklin, Rush recalls a bit of grim humor about the possibility of hanging.

FROM

Dr. Benjamin Rush's Letter to John Adams

1811

Dear Old Friend,

The 4th of July has been celebrated in Philadelphia in the manner I expected. The military men . . . ran away with all the glory of the day. Scarcely a word was said of the **solicitude** and labors and fears and sorrows and sleepless nights of the men who projected, proposed, defended, and **subscribed** the Declaration of Independence.

Do you recollect your memorable speech upon the day on which the vote was taken? Do you recollect the **pensive** and awful silence which **pervaded** the house when we were called up, one after another, to the table of the President of Congress to subscribe what was believed by many at that time to be our death warrants?

The silence and the gloom of the morning were interrupted, I well recollect, only for a moment by Colonel Harrison of Virginia, who said to Mr. Gerry at the table, "I shall have a great advantage over you, Mr. Gerry, when we are all hung for what we are now doing. From the size and weight of my body I shall die in a few minutes, but from the lightness of your body you will dance in the air for an hour or two. . . ." This speech procured a transient smile, but it was soon succeeded by the **solemnity** with which the whole business was conducted.

Celebrating the Declaration

During July and August the Declaration was read in public in town after town throughout America. Everywhere it was received with great celebration. The thirteen colonies had now become the thirteen United States of America.

Celebrating the Declaration of Independence was also an occasion to tear down the statues of King George III that had been erected in 1763 to celebrate victory in the French and Indian War.

"Remember the Ladies"

Abigail Adams, the wife of patriot leader John Adams, wrote to her husband in the spring of 1776, expressing her concerns about the declaration she was sure they would write. Like most colonial women, Abigail had received little formal schooling, but her curiosity and desire to learn had led her to become well informed about the events of the times. Like women throughout America, she could not vote or hold office, but she proved perfectly capable of managing the family's farm south of Boston and even keeping John's law practice going.

Until John became the nation's second president in 1796, the couple were separated by the needs of the Revolution more often than they were together. They kept up a lively—and now famous—correspondence, including the two short selections included here: Abigail's request to "remember the ladies" in the Declaration, and John's response.

FROM

Abigail Adams's Letter to John Adams

MARCH 31, 1776

I long to hear that you have declared an independancy— and by the way in the new Code of Laws which I suppose it will be necessary for you to make I desire you would Remember the Ladies, and be more generous and favourable to them than your ancestors. Do not put such unlimited power into the hands of the Husbands. Remember all Men would be tyrants if they could. If particular care and attention is not paid to the Ladies we are determined to **foment** a Rebelion, and will not hold ourselves bound by any Laws in which we have no voice, or Representation.

That your Sex are Naturally Tyrannical is a Truth so thoroughly established as to admit of no dispute, but such of you as wish to be happy willingly give up the harsh title of Master for the more tender and endearing one of Friend. Why then, not put it out of the power of the vicious and the Lawless to use us with cruelty and indignity with **impunity.** Men of Sense in all Ages **abhor** those customs which treat us only as the **vassals** of your Sex. Regard us then as Beings placed by **providence** under your protection and in immitation of the **Supreem Being** make use of that power only for our happiness.

foment: encourage to grow.

impunity: safe from punishment.

abhor: regard with horror.

vassals: servants or slaves.

providence: God, or divine intervention.

Supreem Being: God.

ぽ ぽ ぽ ぽ ぽ ぽ ぽ ぽ ぽ ぽ ぽ ぽ ぽ ぽ ぽ

FROM

John Adams's Reply

APRIL 14, 1776

Depend upon it, we know better than to repeal our mascu-
line systems. Although they are in full force, you know they
are little more than theory. We dare not use our power to its
full extent. We are obliged to be fair and soft, and in practice, you know, we are the subjects. We have only the title of
masters, and rather than give this up, which would subject
us completely to the despotism of the petticoat, I hope
General Washington and all our brave heroes would fight.

The American Army and Militia

While the Congress was debating the Declaration of Independence in
Philadelphia, a British invasion force had sailed into New York Harbor
and landed on Staten Island. General Washington had been in New York
City since April, and he had a force of about 19,000 men ready to meet
the British. About half this force was made up of militia units from New
York, New Jersey, and New England. These units had little discipline, and
as Washington soon learned, they fought fiercely when their towns were
attacked but tended to run away from any large-scale battles.

To make matters worse, the troops were stunned to see another huge
fleet approaching, larger than the first, 159 ships bringing still more redcoats and 8,000 hired German troops who were called Hessians (from the
German state of Hesse). Washington's 19,000 men were now up against
32,000 British and Germans, and all the waterways were filled with British
warships.

The following reading is from the journal of a Connecticut militia private, Joseph Plumb Martin. After he and his group had waited all night in
a trench, the morning revealed four British warships in the river in front
of them.

The Commander's Fury

A few minutes after the action described by Private Martin, General Washington came upon the retreating militia. He rushed at the officers, shouting and swearing, even striking them with his riding crop. The frightened men continued to flee. A company of Hessians approached and might have shot or captured the general, but one of his aides grabbed the horse's halter and quickly led him to safety. Washington was beginning to learn how much he could expect from militia.

grapeshot: small pellets, like buckshot.

langrage: chunks of scrap metal. Both kinds of ammunition were shot from cannons to spread the damage over a wider area.

F R O M

Private Joseph Martin's Journal

1 7 7 6

As soon as it was fairly light, we saw their boats coming . . . filled with British soldiers. . . . They continued to add to their force until they appeared like a large clover field in full bloom. . . . We lay very quiet in our ditch, waiting their motions. . . .

All of a sudden, there came such a peal of thunder from the British ships that I thought my head would come off. . . .

When our officers saw we would soon be entirely exposed to the rake of their guns, they gave the order to leave the lines.

In retreating we had to cross a level, clear spot of ground, forty or fifty rods wide, exposed to the whole of the enemy's fire. And they gave it to us in prime order. The **grapeshot** and **langrage** flew merrily, which served to quicken our motions. . . .

We had not gone far [in the highway] before we saw a party of men, apparently hurrying on in the same direction with ourselves. We endeavored hard to overtake them, but on approaching them we found . . . they were Hessians. We immediately altered our course and took the main road leading to King's Bridge.

We had not long been on this road before we saw another party, just ahead of us, whom we knew to be Americans. Just as we overtook these, they were fired upon by a party of British from a cornfield, and all was immediately in confusion again. I believe the enemy's party was small, but our people were all militia, and the demons of fear and disorder seemed to take full possession of all and everything on that day. When I came to the spot where the militia were fired upon, the ground was literally covered with arms, knapsacks, staves, coats, hats.

Sergeant Smith's Turkey Prisoners

The battle for New York did not end well for the Americans. In the midst of the battle Washington and his officers realized that it was futile for the Americans to try to take on the redcoats in a full-scale battle. Washington decided that his strategy now would be to keep an army in the field at all times while avoiding a head-on battle, picking his spots for when and where to fight. He managed to get his troops out of New York, keeping his army together and letting the redcoats take the city. The British occupied New York City until the end of the war.

The war settled into a long, grueling struggle, most of the time with no end in sight. Fortunately, there were enough victories to keep the Americans hopeful, and there were lighter moments as well. In the following selection, Sergeant John Smith of the Continental Army tells what happened to a special group of "prisoners" who didn't know the patriot *countersign,* or password.

FROM

Sergeant John Smith's Diary

1776

Sept. 29 [1776]

We kept close to our hut, being obliged to for it Rain'd some part of the Day. This morning at the dock we met mr. William Brown of [Swansea, Mass.] in a sloop loaded with shugar and Rum, by whome we sent Letters home. This evening our . . . Patrole went out & took Up a Sheep & two Large fat turkeys. Since they were not able to Give the Countersign, & were Brought to our Castel, they was tried by fire & Executed By the Whole Division of the free Booters. Then whilst the Feast was Geting Ready, two of our Party . . . found a Boat & Crossed the River [and] found a float [barge] loaded with Oisters, out of which they took about two Bushels . . . & Brought it over to our Castel.

The American Turtle

David Bushnell, the inventor of the *American Turtle*, was too frail to operate the craft. His brother agreed to do it, but he became ill, so Sergeant Lee volunteered.

The submarine was invented by a Connecticut patriot named David Bushnell. During a lull in the battle for New York, General Washington gave permission for the world's first submarine attack. Sergeant Ezra Lee piloted the *American Turtle* against a British warship. In the following selection, Sergeant Lee first describes how the submarine was operated, and then his adventure in New York Harbor near Staten Island.

FROM

Sergeant Ezra Lee's Letter to David Humphrey

1776

Its shape was more like a round clam [than a turtle]. . . . It was high enough to stand in, or sit, as you had occasion with a [metal door plate] hanging on hinges. It had six glasses inserted in the head [door plate] and made water tight, each the size of a half-dollar piece to admit light. . . . The machine was steered by a rudder, having a crooked tiller which led in by your side through a water joint. Then sitting on the seat, the navigator rows with one hand and steers with the other. It had two oars of about twelve inches in length . . . shaped like the arms of a windmill . . . which were worked by means of a **winch;** and with hard labor the machine might be **impelled** at the rate of 3 knots an hour for a short time.

Seven hundred pounds of lead were fixed on the bottom for **ballast,** and two hundred so continued as to let . . . go in case the pumps choked, so that you could rise to the surface. . . .

[After a few experiments, Sergeant Lee was ready.] The moon was about two hours high, and the daylight about one. When I rowed under the stern of the ship, I could see

winch: similar to a crank, which was turned to move the oar.

impelled: pushed, or driven, forward.

ballast: weight placed in the bottom of a boat or ship for balance.

the men on deck and hear them talk. I then shut down all the doors, sunk down, and came under the bottom of the ship. Up with the screw against the bottom, but found that it would not enter [the coppered hull]. I pulled along to try another place, but deviated a little one side and immediately rose with great velocity and came above the surface two or three feet between the ship and the daylight, then sunk again like a porpoise. . . .

[*A British boat approached him.*] I eyed them, and when they had got within fifty or sixty yards of me, I let loose the magazine [bomb] in hopes that if they should take me, they would likewise pick up the magazine and then we should all be blown up together. But as kind Providence would have it, they took fright and returned to the island, to my infinite joy. I then weathered the island, and our people seeing me, came off with a whaleboat and towed me in. The magazine, after getting a little past the island, went off with a tremendous explosion, throwing up large bodies of water to an immense height.

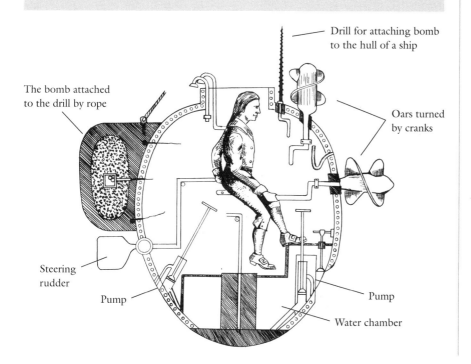

Drill for attaching bomb to the hull of a ship

The bomb attached to the drill by rope

Oars turned by cranks

Steering rudder

Pump

Pump

Water chamber

David Bushnell's submarine the American Turtle, *1776.*

"The Times That Try Men's Souls"

The months following the Declaration of Independence were a dark time for the American cause. After giving up New York City to the British, Washington led his battered army in a desperate retreat across New Jersey. His once-proud Continental Army was now reduced to fewer than four thousand men, their uniforms had become ragged, and some men had no shoes or coats.

Early in December 1776 the Continental Army crossed the Delaware River into Pennsylvania, where they were safe for the time being. Washington had his men collect every boat they could find and bring them all to the Pennsylvania side. To pursue them the British would have to build their own boats or wait for the Delaware to freeze.

Thomas Paine, whose pamphlet *Common Sense* had caused such a stir early in the same year, marched with the army as a volunteer. He wrote another pamphlet, part of a series he called *The American Crisis,* which was being circulated in Philadelphia (and then throughout the thirteen states) while the army was camped on the Delaware. The next selection is from Paine's pamphlet.

FROM

Thomas Paine's The American Crisis
1776

These are the times that try men's souls. The summer soldier and the sunshine patriot will, in this crisis, shrink from the service of their country; but he that stands it *now* deserves the love and thanks of man and woman. Tyranny, like hell, is not easily conquered; yet we have this consolation with us, that the harder the conflict, the more glorious the triumph. What we obtain too cheap, we esteem too lightly: it is dearness only that gives everything its value. Heaven knows how to put a proper price upon its goods; and it would be strange indeed if so celestial an article as FREEDOM should not be highly rated.

*W*ashington's Christmas Surprise

Historians agree that two of the greatest assets the Americans had in their long struggle for independence were the determination of a core group of patriots not to give up, and the leadership of George Washington, which included his ability to inspire his men.

Both of these qualities were critical on Christmas night, 1776, when Washington led his army across the ice-choked Delaware River and attacked a Hessian regiment stationed at Trenton, New Jersey. The Battle of Trenton was a stunning victory for the Americans and restored people's confidence in the patriot cause. A few days later Washington struck again, gaining a dramatic victory over a British force in the Battle of Princeton. These two triumphs drove the British and Hessians out of nearly all of New Jersey.

One of Washington's aides, a young Irish immigrant named Colonel John Fitzgerald, recorded the events of December 25–26 in his journal.

FROM
Colonel John Fitzgerald's Diary
1776

Christmas, 6 P.M.—The regiments have had their evening parade, but instead of returning to their quarters are marching toward the ferry. It is fearfully cold and raw and a snowstorm setting in. The wind is northeast and beats in the faces of the men. It will be a terrible night for the soldiers who have no shoes. Some of them have tied old rags around their feet; others are barefoot, but I have not heard a man complain. They are ready to suffer any hardship and die rather than give up their liberty. I have just copied the order for marching. Both divisions are to go from the ferry to Bear Tavern, two miles. They will separate there; Washington will accompany Greene's division with a part of the artillery down the Pennington road. Sullivan and the rest of the artillery will take the river road.

METROPOLITAN MUSEUM OF ART, GIFT OF JOHN S. KENNEDY, 1897

Painting of Washington and his army crossing the Delaware River on the night of December 25-26, 1776, by Emmanuel Leutze. Leutze painted it in Germany more than half a century after the American Revolution.

Dec. 26, 3 A.M.—I am writing in the ferry house. The troops are all over, and the boats have gone back for the artillery. We are three hours behind the set time. Glover's men have had a hard time to force the boats through the floating ice with the snow drifting in their faces. I never have seen Washington so determined as he is now. He stands on the bank of the river, wrapped in his cloak, superintending the landing of his troops. He is calm and collected, but very determined. The storm is changing to sleet and cuts like a knife. The last cannon is being landed, and we are ready to mount our horses.

Dec. 26, noon—It was nearly four o'clock when we started. The two divisions divided at Bear Tavern. At Birmingham, three and a half miles south of the tavern, a man came with a message from General Sullivan that the storm was wetting the muskets and rendering them unfit for service.

"Tell General Sullivan," said Washington, "to use the bayonet. I am resolved to take Trenton." . . .

[After the battle:] We have taken nearly one thousand prisoners, six cannon, more than one thousand muskets, twelve drums, and four **colors.** About forty Hessians were killed or wounded. Our loss is only two killed and three wounded. Two of the latter are Captain [William] Washington and Lieutenant [James] Monroe, who rushed forward very bravely to seize the cannon. . . .

Dec. 27. It is a glorious victory. It will rejoice the hearts of our friends everywhere and give new life to our hitherto waning fortunes. Washington had baffled the enemy in his retreat from New York. He has pounced upon the Hessians like an eagle upon a hen and is safe once more on this side of the rivers. If he does nothing more, he will live in history as a great military commander.

colors: regimental flags.

The Battle of Saratoga

In one of the major battles of the war, the British and American armies collided in the Battle of Saratoga, fought on two different days—one in September and the other three weeks later, in October 1777. The Americans, under the command of General Horatio Gates, won a spectacular victory, forcing British General John Burgoyne to surrender his entire army, including seven generals, three hundred other officers, and nearly six thousand men.

The Battle of Saratoga was the turning point in the war, even though the conflict continued for four more years. One reason it was so important was that it convinced the government of France that the Americans could win. The French agreed to become America's ally in the war, and even before the French army and navy could send troops, they provided shiploads of weapons and supplies, which proved vital to the cause.

Winter at Valley Forge

Two months after the great victory at Saratoga, Washington led his Continental Army into winter quarters at Valley Forge, a few miles from Philadelphia—which was occupied by the British. The weather was bitterly cold in that winter of 1777–1778, and the eleven thousand men lacked food, adequate clothing, and even blankets. Hundreds died from the cold, starvation, and illnesses like *typhus,* a disease caused by bacteria.

In spite of the hardships, the soldiers did not lose faith in their cause or in Washington. In addition, a German volunteer, Baron von Steuben, spent the winter putting the men through military drills. By spring the troops had formed a disciplined army, filled with a new confidence and eager to take on the British.

The following reading, from the diary of Dr. Albigence Waldo, a surgeon from Connecticut, describes the hardships of the first month in Valley Forge.

FROM
The Diary of Dr. Albigence Waldo
1777–1778

Dec. 12th We are ordered to march over the river—it snows—I'm sick—eat nothing—no whiskey—no baggage—Lord—Lord—Lord. The army were till sunrise crossing the river—some at the wagon bridge and some at the raft bridge below. Cold and uncomfortable. . . .

Dec. 14th Poor food—hard lodging—cold weather—fatigue—nasty clothes—nasty cookery—vomit half my time—smoked out of my senses—the Devil's in it—I can't endure it—why are we sent here to starve and freeze. . . . Here comes a bowl of beef soup—full of burnt leaves and dirt . . . away with it Boys—I'll live like the chameleon on air. . . .

December 21, 1777. Preparations made for huts. Provisions scarce. Heartily wish myself at home. My skin and eyes are almost spoiled with continual smoke. A general cry through the camp this evening among the soldiers: "No meat! No meat!"

$\mathcal{B}$enedict Arnold: "Treason of the Blackest Dye"

Benedict Arnold had been one of America's most courageous and successful generals. In 1775–1776 he had nearly succeeded in capturing Quebec, and in 1777 he was a hero of the Battle of Saratoga. In June 1778, as a gesture to General Arnold for his heroism at Saratoga, Washington made him military governor of Philadelphia.

Arnold enjoyed his new position. He hired a staff of personal servants and began giving lavish dinner parties for leading Philadelphians. He courted, then married, eighteen-year-old Peggy Shippen, of a wealthy Philadelphia family.

Late in 1779 charges were brought against Arnold by the Pennsylvania government for several illegal activities, including selling the goods left behind by loyalists, and he faced a court-martial. The military court found him guilty on only two of eight charges, and the only punishment was a reprimand by General Washington. But even the rather mild rebuke he received from the great commander-in-chief humiliated and angered him.

A few weeks after the reprimand Arnold made his first secret contacts with the British, indicating his interest in being a traitor. No one knows how much of Arnold's decision was due to the humiliation of the trial and how much was due to his constant need for money. Peggy was also an influence. She had been very popular among the British in Philadelphia, and one of her friends from those days, Major John André, became the go-between for Arnold and the British commander in New York, General Henry Clinton.

Arnold next persuaded Washington to place him in charge of West Point, the Americans' most important fort, on the Hudson River north of New York City. Then, through letters written in code, he arranged to turn the fort over to the British in exchange for a large sum of money and a commission in the British army.

The scheme might have succeeded except for some unusual circumstances. First, André and Arnold had a meeting near West Point; as Arnold returned to the fort he learned that Washington and his staff were on their way to visit West Point. While Arnold waited calmly at breakfast for Washington's arrival, a messenger arrived with the shocking news that the patriot militia had captured André.

The following selection is General Nathaniel Greene's announcement of the plot's discovery.

The Fate of Peggy and Benedict Arnold

Although Arnold failed to deliver West Point, he did receive money from the British and was made a general. He soon led violent raids against the Americans in Virginia and Connecticut, burning houses and other buildings. In 1781 he and Peggy went to England, where they remained for the rest of their lives—except for a short time in Canada. Arnold struggled to restore his fortune and his reputation but was never very successful and he died a bitter man. Peggy remained loyal to him to the end, even paying off his debts.

Caricature of Benedict Arnold being hung in effigy, from the Continental Almanack, *1781.*

METROPOLITAN MUSEUM OF ART, BEQUEST OF CHARLES ALLEN MUNN, 1924

providential: resulting from divine intervention.

⚜ ⚜ ⚜ ⚜ ⚜ ⚜ ⚜ ⚜ ⚜ ⚜ ⚜ ⚜ ⚜ ⚜

FROM

General Nathaniel Greene's Announcement to the Continental Army

SEPTEMBER 16, 1780

Treason of the blackest dye was yesterday discovered. General Arnold, who commanded at West Point, lost to every sentiment of honor, of private and public obligation, was about to deliver up that important post into the hands of the enemy. Such an event must have given the American cause a dangerous, if not a fatal wound. Happily the treason has been timely discovered. . . . The **providential** train of circumstances which led to it affords the most convincing proofs that the liberties of America are the object of divine protection. . . . Great honor is due to the American army that this is the first instance of treason of the kind, where many were to be expected from the nature of our dispute.

John André, a handsome young actor and playwright, was not in uniform when he was captured, and so he was executed as a spy, not as a soldier. He had hoped that Washington would let him be shot by a firing squad, as a soldier would have been, but the general denied the request.

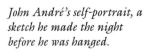

John André's self-portrait, a sketch he made the night before he was hanged.

Communicating in Code

In every war since the time of Julius Caesar, spies have used *ciphers,* or secret codes, to communicate with their contact without being detected. Benedict Arnold and Major André used a simple system that required both Arnold and a loyalist named Joseph Stansbury to have a copy of Blackstone's *Commentaries on the Laws of England.* Each word in a letter was represented by three numbers: the first number referred to a page in the book; the second number to the line on the page, and the third number was the place of the word in the line. For example, if Arnold wrote "16, 4, 7," Stansbury would know to find the seventh word on the fourth line of page 16 in Blackstone's book. If anyone had discovered the book they were using, the code could have been easily broken.

The Turn toward Victory

From the autumn of 1780, the British force in the South under Lord Cornwallis fought and won several battles with the patriots. But each victory weakened the British. Eventually Cornwallis was forced to retreat to the Yorktown peninsula in Virginia.

The fate of the British was actually sealed by two impressive patriot victories on the frontier between North and South Carolina—one at King's Mountain in November 1780 and the other at Cowpens in January 1781. A young militia private, sixteen-year-old James Collins, had his first taste of battle at King's Mountain. Here is how he described the experience.

FROM

James Collins's Journal

1780

Here I confess I would willingly have been excused . . . but I could not well swallow the **appellation** of coward. . . . We were soon in motion, every man throwing four or five [musket] balls in his mouth to prevent thirst—also to be in readiness to reload quick. The shot of the enemy soon began to pass over us like hail. . . . I was soon in a **profuse** sweat. My lot happened to be in the center, where the severest part of the battle was fought. We soon attempted to climb the hill, but were fiercely charged upon and forced to fall back to our first position. We tried a second time, but met the same fate. The fight then seemed to become more furious. . . . We took to the hill a third time. The enemy gave way. When we had gotten near the top, some of our leaders roared out, "Hurrah, my brave fellows! Advance! They are crying for **quarter**!" By this time . . . the enemy was completely hemmed in on all sides, and no chance of escaping. Besides, their leader [Patrick Ferguson] had fallen. They soon threw down their arms and surrendered.

appellation: name or title.
profuse: pouring forth.
quarter: mercy.

The Battle of Cowpens, January 17, 1781

At a grazing area called the Cowpens, Continental General Daniel Morgan faced a British force that outnumbered his by more than two to one. In addition, one-third of Morgan's men were inexperienced militiamen. His brilliant battle plan, shown on the map here, turned a likely defeat into a stunning victory.

Morgan knew his militiamen, commanded by Colonel Andrew Pickens, were likely to panic, so he put them in the front line with orders to take one or two shots, then retreat behind a hill to the rear. Behind the militia, Morgan stationed a line of Continental veterans under Colonel Howard. On their left flank, Morgan placed some of his best sharpshooters, and in the rear, a cavalry unit under Colonel William Washington.

The redcoats advanced directly into Morgan's trap, while he stayed with the militia, calming them as they took their shots then scurried to the safety of the hill. The British and loyalists, convinced that the patriot lines were crumbling, rushed ahead, only to be stopped by Howard's Continentals.

Morgan then had the cavalry attack one flank while Pickens reorganized the militia to attack the other flank. The British panicked, and those who could get away fled. They left behind more than three hundred killed or wounded and five hundred prisoners. The patriots suffered only twelve killed and sixty wounded.

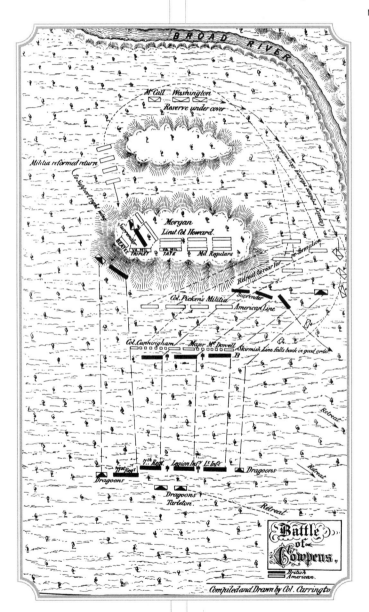

Map of the Battle of Cowpens.

The Victory at Yorktown

Lord Cornwallis thought he was in a strong position at Yorktown in Virginia, where he could wait for the British fleet to bring more troops and supplies. But General Washington made a series of brilliant moves. While his southern army kept Cornwallis at Yorktown, Washington raced south with his Continentals and a French army under Count Rochambeau. At the same time Washington had the French fleet block the British fleet from reaching Cornwallis.

Washington's plan worked perfectly. By late September 1781 Cornwallis, with eight thousand men, found himself hemmed in by nine thousand Americans and nearly eight thousand French. After three weeks of bombardment, Cornwallis surrendered with his army on October 19, 1781.

In the following reading, young Dr. James Thacher (see page 82) describes the final days and the surrender at Yorktown.

The End of the Revolution

The victory at Yorktown ended the war. The British still had an army in New York, but the British government, the people, and the troops had had enough. Between the Battles of Yorktown and Saratoga, the British had lost two entire armies to the Americans. The Americans now had the full support of the French army and navy. Lord North, the king's minister in Parliament who had conducted the war, resigned, and the king's new minister immediately sent peace commissioners to Paris to discuss terms with both American and French negotiators. The peace treaty was finally approved and signed early in 1783.

A French engraving of the Battle of Yorktown.

FROM
James Thacher's Journal
1781

[October 17, 1781] The whole of our **works** are now mounted with cannon and mortars. Not less than one hundred pieces of heavy **ordnance** have been in continual operation during the last twenty-four hours. The whole peninsula trembles under the incessant thunderings of our infernal machines. We have leveled some of their works in ruins and silenced their guns. They have almost ceased firing. We are so near as to have a distinct view of the dreadful havoc and destruction of their works, and even see the men in their lines tore to pieces by the bursting of our shells. But the scene is drawing to a close. Lord Cornwallis, at length realizing the extreme hazard of his deplorable situation and finding it in vain any longer to resist, has. . . come to the humiliating expedient of sending out a flag requesting a cessation of hostilities for twenty-four hours that commissioners may be appointed to prepare and adjust the terms of **capitulation.** 19th: This is to us a most glorious day; but to the English [one] of bitter chagrin and disappointment. . . . At about twelve o'clock the combined [Franco-American] army was arranged and drawn in two lines extending more than a mile in length. The Americans were drawn up in a line on the right side of the road, and the French occupied the left. At the head of the former, the great American commander [Washington], mounted on his noble courser, took his station attended by his aids. At the head of the latter was posted the excellent Count Rochambeau and his **suite.** The French troops, in complete uniform, displayed a martial and noble appearance. The band of music, of which the **timbrel** formed a part, is a delightful novelty, and produced, while marching to the ground, a most enchanting effect. The Americans, though not all in uniform nor their dress so neat, yet exhibited an erect soldierly air, and every countenance beamed with satisfaction and joy. The **concourse** of spectators from the country was **prodigious**. . . but universal silence and order prevailed.

Primitive painting of Washington and Lafayette at the Battle of Yorktown, by Reuben Law Reed, c. 1860.

works: defenses such as trenches and log barriers.

ordnance: weapons and ammunition.

capitulation: surrender.

suite: a complete set—in this case, a staff of officers.

timbrel: an ancient form of a tambourine.

concourse: a broad, open space.

prodigious: mighty, large.

PART VI

CREATING A NATIONAL GOVERNMENT

When the Continental Congress issued the Declaration of Independence in July 1776, the thirteen former British colonies became the thirteen United States. The Congress urged each state to write its own constitution— the framework of laws that described how the government would operate. Each state soon had its own constitution, and the people of each state were proud of their independence.

The Continental Congress had guided America through the Revolution. The Congress, however, was not a true national government because it lacked important powers. For example, it did not have the power to tax; it could only ask the states to contribute the amounts needed. The state governments did contribute, but never as much as the Congress needed. One result was that, when the war ended, the Congress had a huge debt, including the back pay it owed to the soldiers and their officers.

During the war the members of the Congress had drawn up a framework of government for the nation—called the Articles of Confederation—in which the national government had few powers. But by 1786 many Americans had realized that the Confederation government was too weak to hold the states together. At times warfare between two or more states seemed likely. Some people—in Europe as well as in America—predicted that the union of states would soon dissolve into thirteen warring states, or that larger states would take over smaller ones. Others predicted that some form of monarchy would emerge from the failure of the Confederation. In 1787 the country's leaders agreed to hold a Constitutional Convention—a meeting of delegates from all the states to revise the Articles of Confederation. Instead, the delegates created an entirely new framework—the Constitution of the United States, which we continue to live under today.

What Form of Government?

Even before independence was declared in July 1776, many Americans wondered what kind of government would replace rule by Britain's king and Parliament. In the next selection, Abigail Adams raised such questions in a letter to her husband John, who was on the committee chosen to draft the Declaration of Independence.

FROM

Abigail Adams's Letter to John Adams

1776

I wish I knew what mighty things were fabricating. If a form of government is to be established here, what one will be assumed? Will it be left to our assemblies to choose one? And will not many people have many minds? And shall we not run into dissensions among ourselves?

The building up of a great empire may now I suppose be realized even by the unbelievers. Yet will not ten thousand difficulties arise in the formation of it? The reins of government have been so long slackened, that I fear the people will not quietly submit to those restraints which are necessary for the peace, and security, of the community.

If we separate from Britain, what code of laws will be established? How shall we be governed so as to retain our liberties? Can any government be free which is not administered by general stated laws? Who shall frame these laws? Who will give them force and energy?. . .

When I consider these things . . . I feel anxious for the fate of our monarchy or democracy or whatever is to take place.

Shays' Rebellion

In the winter of 1786–1787, Massachusetts was rocked by an armed rebellion of farmers who had fought in the Revolution. Many were losing their farms because they could not pay their taxes, and they insisted they were in debt only because they had not been paid for their years of military service. Led by Daniel Shays, a former captain, they surrounded courthouses and commanded judges to stop seizing their property to pay their taxes. When Shays led 1,200 men in an attempt to seize the arsenal in Springfield, the Massachusetts militia drove them off, then hunted down dozens and arrested them.

One important result of Shays' Rebellion was that it convinced leaders in many states that a stronger government was needed. The soldiers had not been paid because the Congress had no money; without the power to raise taxes, the Congress could only ask the states to contribute.

Included here are a petition by a group of farmers to the Massachusetts government and a newspaper interview with one of the farmers.

FROM

A Farmers' Petition to the State Government

SUMMER 1786

We beg to inform your Honors that unless something takes place more favorable to the people, in a little time at least, one half of our inhabitants in our opinion will become bankrupt. . . . Surely your Honors are not strangers to the distresses of the people, but do know that many of our good inhabitants are now confined in jail for debt and taxes; many have fled, others wishing to flee to the state of New York or some other state.

FROM

An Interview in the Massachusetts Centinal

OCTOBER 25, 1786

He said, "We all have grievances enough; I can tell you mine. I have labored hard all my days, and fared hard. I have been greatly abused, been obliged to do more than my part in the war, been loaded with class-rates, town-rates, province-rates, continental-rates, and all rates [taxes], lawsuits, and have been pulled and hauled by sheriffs, constables, and collectors, and had my cattle sold for less than they were worth. I have been obliged to pay, and nobody will pay me. I have lost a great deal by this man and that man and t'other man, and the great men are going to get all we have, and I think it is time for us to rise and put a stop to it, and have no more courts, nor sheriffs, nor collectors, nor lawyers. I design to pay no more, and I know we have the biggest party, let them say what they will."

The Meeting of the Constitutional Convention

In May 1787, fifty-five delegates from every state but Rhode Island were chosen to go to the Constitutional Convention in Philadelphia. In the following selection, Major William Pierce describes three of the most famous delegates—Benjamin Franklin, George Washington, and James Madison. Major Pierce was a delegate from Georgia.

FROM

Major William Pierce's Notes

1787

Doctor Franklin is well known to be the greatest philosopher of the present age. All the operations of nature he seems to understand. The very heavens obey him. The clouds yield up their lightning to be imprisoned in his lightning rod. But what claim he has to be a politician, the future must determine. It is certain that he does not shine much in public council. He is no public speaker. Nor does he seem to let politics engage his attention.

He is, however, a very unusual man. He tells a story in a style more charming than anything I have ever heard. He is eighty-two years old and his active mind is equal to that of a youth of twenty-five years of age. . . .

General Washington is well known as the commander in chief of the late American army. Having

Engraved portrait of Benjamin Franklin, after a painting by D. Martin.

METROPOLITAN MUSEUM OF ART, BEQUEST OF CHARLES ALLEN MUNN, 1924

Invaders Limited to Three Thousand Troops

Because many delegates in the Convention worried about giving too much power to the president, the suggestion was made that the armed forces could contain no more than three thousand men.

General Washington said he would agree if the Constitution also stated that no enemy could invade America with more than three thousand troops.

brought these states to independence and peace, he now comes to assist in framing a government. Like Cincinnatus [a Roman general], he returned to his farm perfectly contented with being only a plain citizen. After enjoying the highest honor of the confederation, now he only seeks the approval of his countrymen by being virtuous and useful. . . .

Mr. Madison has long been in public life. What is very remarkable, every person seems to admit his greatness. He blends together the politician and the scholar. In the management of every great question, he evidently took the lead in the Convention.

Though he cannot be called an orator, he is a most agreeable and convincing speaker. He possesses a spirit of hard work and deep study. He always comes forward the best-informed person of any point in a debate. In relation to the affairs of the United States, he perhaps has the most correct knowledge of anyone in the Union. He has twice been a member of Congress and was always thought one of its ablest members. Mr. Madison is about thirty-seven years of age. He is easy and unreserved among people he knows and has a most agreeable style of conversation.

His Excellency, General Washington

General Washington was as much a legend in his own day as he was to later generations. As the man who led America to independence, many in Europe thought he would soon make himself king or emperor, and people often referred to him as "His Excellency," rather than as "the General." He had no such ambitions and was only too happy to return to his plantation, Mount Vernon.

Washington was the presiding officer of the Convention, and he made sure there were no unruly arguments or shouting matches; just a glance from the General was enough to silence anyone.

Jefferson's Macaroni Machine

In 1785, Thomas Jefferson was sent to France as America's ambassador. Although he was absent for the crucial debates on forming a government, he wrote to Madison and others expressing his thoughts on the subject. As he traveled throughout Europe he found countless products and ways of doing things he thought would be useful in America. One of his discoveries was a macaroni machine. His drawing and description of the machine are pictured here.

Jefferson's drawing of a macaroni machine and instructions on how to make pasta, c. 1787.

Maccaroni.

The best maccaroni in Italy is made with a particular sort of flour called Semola, in Naples: but in almost every shop a different sort of flour is commonly used; for, provided the flour be of a good quality & not ground extremely fine, it will always do very well. a paste is made with flour, water & less yeast than is used for making bread. this paste is then put, by little at a time viz. about 5. or 6.℔ each time into a round iron box ABC. the under part of which is perforated with holes, through which the paste when pressed by the screw DEF. comes out, and forms the Maccaroni ggg. which, then sufficiently long, are cut & spread to dry. the screw is turned by a lever inserted into the hole K. of which there are 4. or 6. it is evident that on turning the screw one way, the cylindrical part F which fits the iron box or mortar perfectly well, must press upon the paste and must force it out of the holes. I.LM. is a strong wooden frame, properly fastened to the wall, floor & cieling of the room.
N.O. is a figure on a larger scale, of some of the holes in the iron plate, where all the black is solid, and the rest open. the real plate has a great many holes, and is screwed to the box or mortar: or rather there is a set of plates which may be changed at will, with holes of different shapes & sizes for the different sorts of Maccaroni.

Surviving Philadelphia's Summer

One of the greatest difficulties the delegates faced was the heat of Philadelphia's summer. In order to have quiet and to keep their deliberations secret, the windows of the State House were nailed shut. Several heat waves, one that lasted nine days, added to the suffering of that summer. Some historians think the uncomfortable conditions made negotiations go faster.

A French visitor had this impression of that summer.

FROM

A French Visitor's Description of Philadelphia in Summer

1787

A veritable torture during Philadelphia's hot season is the innumerable flies which constantly light on the face and hands, stinging everywhere. . . . Rooms must be kept closed unless one wishes to be tormented in his bed . . . and this makes the heat of the night even more unbearable and sleep more difficult.

The Constitution

The work of the Convention was completed in about ten weeks. After a committee on style smoothed out the wording and added a preamble, the completed Constitution was read to the Convention. Of the forty-two men present, thirty-nine signed the document. The three who refused did so because the document did not spell out the rights and freedoms of individuals. The need to add statements on those rights and freedoms came up again as the states debated whether to ratify the new Constitution. The framers agreed that, as soon as the Constitution was *ratified*, or accepted, by the special conventions to be held in each state, a Bill of Rights would be added as the first amendments to the document.

The Constitution has served the nation for well over two hundred years, as the United States has grown from less than 3 million people to nearly 300 million today. British statesman William Gladstone called it "the most wonderful work ever struck off at a given time by the brain and purpose of man," and it has inspired more than one hundred other nations in creating frameworks of government.

One reason for the great success of the Constitution has been its flexibility. The framers did not try to spell out in detail all the rules Americans would need in the years ahead. Instead, they provided broad statements of the government's powers and the limits on those powers. They also divided the government into three branches—the legislative, executive, and judicial—and established ways for each branch to check and balance the powers of the others. In addition, provisions were made for *amending,* or changing, the document, but the framers made the process difficult enough that amendments have been added only after careful deliberation.

What follows is a shortened version of the document; some of the wording has been changed to make it easier to understand.

FROM

The Constitution

1788

Preamble

We the people of the United States, in order to form a more perfect Union, establish justice, insure domestic tranquility, provide for the common defense, promote the general welfare, and secure the blessings of liberty to ourselves and our posterity, do ordain and establish this Constitution for the United States of America.

Article 1 [The Legislative Branch]

SECTION 1

All legislative powers herein granted shall be vested in a Congress of the United States, which shall consist of a Senate and a House of Representatives.

SECTION 2 [The House of Representatives]

The House of Representatives shall be composed of members chosen [every two years] by the people of the . . . States. . . .

[The number of representatives from each state shall be based on the state's population.]

SECTION 3 [The Senate]

The Senate of the United States shall be composed of two senators from each State, [chosen] for six years. [At first senators were elected by the state legislatures; this was changed by the Seventeenth Amendment, ratified in 1913, leaving the election to the voters of each state. Every two years one-third of the senators leave office or stand for reelection.]

The Vice President serves as president of the Senate, but votes only in case of a tie.

SECTIONS 4–6 [These sections deal with the organization of the House and Senate.]

SECTION 7 [How a Bill Becomes a Law]

All bills for raising revenue shall originate in the House of Representatives; but the Senate may propose or concur with amendments as on other bills.

Every bill which shall have passed the House of Representatives and the Senate shall, before it become a law, be presented to the President of the United States; if he approve he shall sign it, but if not he shall *return* it [veto it], with objections to that house in which it originated, who shall. . . proceed to reconsider it. . . . If approved by two thirds of [both] houses, it shall become a law. . . . If any bill shall not be returned by the President within ten days . . . [it] shall be a law . . . as if he had signed it, unless the Congress by their adjournment prevent its return, in which case it shall not be a law.

SECTION 8 [Powers Granted to Congress]

The Congress shall have power

To lay and collect taxes . . .

To borrow money . . .

To regulate commerce with foreign nations, and among the several states . . .

To establish an uniform rule of naturalization . . .

To coin money . . . [and] provide for the punishment of counterfeiting . . .

To establish post offices . . .

To encourage authors and inventors by copyrights and patents . . .

To establish needed courts below the Supreme Court . . .

To declare war . . . [and to] raise and support armies . . . and a navy . . .

To provide for calling forth the militia [now called the National Guard] . . .

To make laws regarding federal property. . . .

SECTION 9 [Powers Denied to Congress]

[Among the powers denied to Congress are the power to tax individuals unfairly, to tax exports (goods sent out of a state), and to create titles of nobility.

Article 2 [The Executive Branch]

SECTION 1 [The Offices of the President and Vice President]

The executive power shall be vested in a President of the United States of America. He shall hold his office during the term of four years. . . .

[The electoral college elects the president and vice president. At first the electors were chosen by state legislatures; after 1800 the states gradually shifted to having the voters choose the electors.]

SECTION 2 [Powers Granted to the President]

The President shall be commander in chief of the army and navy of the United States and of the militia of the several States. . . . He shall have power to grant reprieves and pardons. . . .

He shall have power . . . to make treaties, provided two-thirds of the Senators concur [agree]. . . . and he shall nominate. . . . [and] appoint ambassadors. . . .

SECTION 3 [Duties of the President]

He shall from time to time give to the Congress information of the state of the Union [the State of the Union message delivered to Congress each January], and recommend to their consideration such measures as he shall judge necessary and expedient; he may, on extraordinary occasions, convene both houses, or either of them. . . . He shall receive ambassadors and other public ministers; he shall take care that the laws be faithfully executed. . . .

Article 3 [The Judicial Branch]

SECTION 1 [Federal Courts]

The judicial power of the United States shall be vested in one Supreme Court, and in such inferior [lower] courts as the Congress . . . may establish. . . .

SECTION 2 [Jurisdiction of Federal Courts]

The judicial power shall extend to all cases . . . arising under this Constitution. [This has been interpreted to mean that the Supreme Court can declare a law unconstitutional.]

SECTION 3 [Treason]

Treason against the United States shall consist only in levying [waging] war against them. . . . No person shall be convicted of treason unless on the testimony of two witnesses to the same overt act [one that can be seen], or on confession in open court.

The Bill of Rights

The one issue that nearly defeated the Constitution during the debates over ratification was the failure to include a Bill of Rights in the original document. A Bill of Rights, designed to protect individual liberties from an overbearing government, had been written into all of the state constitutions. The framers of the Constitution promised that the first act of the new government would be to add a Bill of Rights as the first ten amendments. This was enough to convince voters at the ratifying conventions to approve the Constitution. The ten amendments were proposed in 1789, and all were ratified in 1791.

Amendments can be proposed in either of two ways: by a two-thirds vote of both the House and Senate, or by a special convention demanded by two-thirds of the states. The second method has not yet been used. Once an amendment has been proposed, there are two ways to ratify it: by the vote of three-fourths of the state legislatures, or of special conventions in three-fourths of the states.

The full text of the Bill of Rights is included here.

The Bill of Rights, Amendments 1–10

1791

Amendment 1

Congress shall make no law respecting an establishment of religion, or prohibiting the free exercise thereof; or abridging the freedom of speech, or of the press; or the right of the people peaceably to assemble, and to petition the government for a redress of grievances.

Amendment 2

A well-regulated militia being necessary to the security of a free State, the right of the people to keep and bear arms shall not be infringed.

Amendment 3

No soldier shall, in time of peace, be quartered in any house without the consent of the owner, nor in time of war, but in a manner to be prescribed by law.

Amendment 4

The right of the people to be secure in their persons, houses, papers, and effects, against unreasonable searches and seizures, shall not be violated, and no warrants shall issue but upon probable cause, supported by oath or affirmation, and particularly describing the place to be searched, and the persons or things to be seized.

Amendment 5

No person shall be held to answer for a capital, or otherwise infamous crime, unless on a presentment or indictment of a grand jury, except in cases arising in the land or naval forces, or in the militia, when in actual service in time of war or public danger; nor shall any person be subject for the same offense to be twice put in jeopardy of life or limb; nor shall be compelled in any criminal case to be a witness against himself, nor be deprived of life, liberty, or property, without due process of law; nor shall private property be taken for public use without just compensation.

Amendment 6

In all criminal prosecutions, the accused shall enjoy the right to a speedy and public trial, by an impartial jury of the State and district wherein the crime shall have been committed, which district shall have been previously ascertained by law, and to be informed of the nature and cause of the accusation; to be confronted with the witnesses against him; to have compulsory process for obtaining witnesses in his favor, and to have the assistance of counsel for his defense.

Amendment 7

In suits at common law, where the value in controversy shall exceed twenty dollars, the right of trial by jury shall be preserved, and no fact tried by a jury shall be otherwise reexamined in any court of the United States, than according to the rules of the common law.

Amendment 8

Excessive bail shall not be required, nor excessive fines imposed, nor cruel and unusual punishments inflicted.

Amendment 9

The enumeration in the Constitution, of certain rights, shall not be construed to deny or disparage others retained by the people.

Amendment 10

The powers not delegated to the United States by the Constitution, nor prohibited by it to the States, are reserved to the States respectively, or to the people.

SOURCES

PART I: Colonizing a New World

An Agreement between Christopher Columbus and the Rulers of Spain, April 17, 1492: adapted from Charles Gibson, ed., *The Spanish Tradition in America* (New York: Harper & Row, 1968), pp. 27–29.

Christopher Columbus's Letter to Lord Raphael Sanchez, March 14, 1493: from R. H. Major, ed., *Selected Letters of Christopher Columbus*, 1847, reprinted in Robert C. Cotner et al., eds., *Readings in American History*, vol. 1, *1492 to 1865* (Boston: Houghton Mifflin, 1976), p. 2.

John White's Journals, 1590: adapted from *John White's Diary, Fourth Voyage*, reprinted in John Berger and Dorothy Berger, eds., *Diary of America* (New York: Simon & Schuster, 1957), pp. 12–20.

John Smith, *A General History of Virginia*, 1624: from *The Annals of America*, vol. 1, *1493–1754, Discovering a New World* (Chicago: Encyclopedia Britannica, 1969), pp. 25–26.

William Bradford, *History of Plymouth Plantation, "The Mayflower Compact,"* 1620–1647: from the edition edited by William Paget, vol. 1 (New York: E. P. Dutton, 1957), pp. 177, 189–193.

William Bradford, *History of Plymouth Plantation*, 1620–1647: from Samuel Eliot Morison, ed., *Of Plymouth Plantation, 1620–1647* (New York: Alfred A. Knopf, 1963), p. 23f.

A German Immigrant's Letter Home, 1750: from Gottlieb Mittelberger, *Journey to Pennsylvania*, edited and translated by Oscar Handlin and John Clive (Cambridge, Mass.: Harvard University Press, 1960), p. 11f.

Forefathers' Song, c. 1630: from *The Annals of America*, vol. 1, p. 116f.

Aulkey Hubertse's Indenture Contract, 1710: from Alice Morse Earle, *Colonial Days in Old New York* (New York: Charles Scribner's Sons, 1896), pp. 84–86.

William Penn, *Some Further Account of the Province of Pennsylvania in America*, 1683: from David C. King et al., *United States History: Readings and Documents* (Menlo Park, Calif.: Addison-Wesley, 1986), p. 12.

London, 1798; quoted from the reprint edition (New York Times/Arno Press, 1973), pp. 188f.

The New England Primer, c. 1680: from *The Annals of America*, vol. 1, p. 276.

George Washington, *Rules of Civility & Decent Behaviour*, 1747: facsimile edition (Bedford, Mass.: Applewood Books), pp. 10 passim.

Reverend John Schuyler's Journal, c. 1805: adapted from the pamphlet *Sartorial Splendor in Colonial New York* (Cooperstown, N.Y.: New York State Historical Society, 1964), p. 16.

A 1710 Description of Dress: from Holliday, *Woman's Life in Colonial Days*, p. 154.

Transcript of the Trial of Sarah Good, 1692: from Emily Davie, ed., *Profile of America: An Autobiography of the U.S.* (New York: Thomas Y. Crowell, 1954), pp. 94–95.

Judge Samuel Sewall's *Diary*, 1696 and 1697: adapted from Berger and Berger, *Diary of America*, pp. 34f.

Anne Bradstreet, "To My Dear and Loving Husband," 1678: from *The Annals of America*, vol. 1, p. 198.

A Letter by Eliza Lucas, 1740: from Mary R. Beard, ed., *America through Women's Eyes* (New York: Macmillan, 1933), pp. 33–34.

The *Royal American Magazine*, 1774: from Clarence L. Ver Steeg, *American Spirit* (Chicago: Follett, 1982), p. 281.

John Winthrop, *History of New England*, 1645: from Beard, *America through Women's Eyes*, p. 90.

The Diary of John Adams, 1775: from Holliday, *Woman's Life in Colonial Days*, p. 109.

Anna Green Winslow's Diary, 1772: from the edition edited by Alice Morse Earle (Boston, 1894), reprinted in Berger and Berger, *Diary of America*, pp. 82f.

The Autobiography of Benjamin Franklin, 1793: from the edition edited by Leonard W. Labaree et al. (New Haven, Conn.: Yale University Press, 1964), pp. 62f.

J. Hector St. Jean de Crevecoeur, *Letters from an American Farmer*, c. 1782: from Thomas A. Bailey, ed., *The American Spirit: United States History as Seen by Contemporaries* (Boston: Heath, 1963), pp. 81–82.

PART II: Daily Life in Colonial America

A Girl's Diary, 1775: from Carl Holliday, *Woman's Life in Colonial Days* (Boston: Cornhill, 1922; reprint, Mineola, NY: Dover, 1999), p. 171.

Andrew Burnaby, *Travels through the Middle Settlements of North America in 1759 and 1760*, 1759: first published in

PART III: Many People, Many Voices

Philip Vickers Fithian's Journal, 1773: from *The Journal and Letters of Philip Vickers Fithian, a Plantation Tutor of the Old Dominion* (Williamsburg, Va.: Colonial Williamsburg, Inc., 1965), pp. 38–39.

J. Hector St. Jean de Crevecoeur, *Letters from an American Farmer, c.* 1782: (New York: Penguin Books, 1981), p. 161.

Equiano's Travels, 1789: from William Loren Katz, ed., *Eyewitness: The Negro in American History* (Belmont, Calif.: David S. Lake Publisher, 1974), p. 124.

"A Slave's Epitaph," 1773: from King et al., *United States History,* p. 128.

Jefferson's Ad for the Return of a Runaway, 1769: from the New York Public Library picture collection.

Jefferson's *Notes on the State of Virginia* 1784: from Julian P. Boyd, ed., *The Papers of Thomas Jefferson,* vol. 1 (Princeton, N.J.: Princeton University Press, 1950), p. 314.

Jefferson's Letter to Frances Epps, 1787: ibid., vol. 11, p. 653.

John White's Journals, 1585: from Sellers, et al., *As It Happened,* p. 112.

A Narrative of the Life of Mrs. Mary Jemison, 1824: from the edition edited by James E. Seaver (New York: Corinth Books, 1960), p. 132.

Andrew Hamilton's Speech in the *Trial of John Peter Zenger,* 1735: from Stanley Katz, ed., *A Brief Narrative of the Case and Trial of John Peter Zenger by James Alexander* (Cambridge, Mass.: Harvard University Press, 1963), pp. 95f.

PART IV: Prelude to Revolution

Pennsylvania Journal and Weekly Advertiser, October 31, 1765: from Dover Pictorial Archives, *The American Revolution* (Mineola, N.Y.: Dover Publishing Co., 1975), p. 1.

The Proceedings of the Congress, October 1765: from *The Annals of America,* vol. 2, 1755–1783, Resistance and Revolution, p. 159.

John Dickinson, *Letters from a Pennsylvania Farmer,* 1768: from David Rothman and Sheila Rothman, *Sources of the American Social Tradition* (New York: Basic Books, 1975), p. 68.

John Tudor's Diary, 1770: from Richard B. Morris and James Woodress, eds., *The Times That Tried Men's Souls* (St. Louis, Mo.: Webster Publishing Co., 1961), p. 226.

Captain Thomas Preston's Letter to a Friend, 1770: from Ver Steeg, *American Spirit,* p. 266.

A Letter by John Andrews, 1773: adapted from Winthrop Sargeant, ed., "Letters of John Andrews, Esq. of Boston, 1772–1776," in Massachusetts Historical Society, *Proceedings,* vol. 8 (Boston: 1866); reprinted in People's Bicentennial Commission, *Voices of the American Revolution* (New York: Bantam Books, 1975), p. 31.

John Adams's Diary, 1773: from L. H. Butterfield, ed., *Diary and Autobiography of John Adams,* vol. 2 (Cambridge, Mass.: Harvard University Press, 1962), pp. 85–86.

Patrick Henry's Speech to the Virginia Assembly, 1775: from *The Annals of America,* vol. 2, p. 323.

PART V: The American Revolution

Paul Revere's Letter to Dr. Jeremy Belknap, 1798: adapted from Henry Steele Commager and Richard B. Morris, eds., *The Spirit of Seventy-Six* (New York: Harper & Row, 1969), pp. 168ff.

Ebenezer Munroe's Diary, 1775: from ibid., p. 188.

Thomas Thorp's Journal, 1775: from Richard Wheeler, *Voices of 1776* (New York: Penguin, 1991), p. 12.

Military Journal of Dr. James Thacher, 1775: from James Thacher, *Military Journal of the American Revolution* (Hartford, Conn.: Hulbert, Williams & Co., 1962; reprint, New York: New York Times/Arno Press, 1969), p. 47.

George Washington's Letter to Martha Washington (Patsy), 1775: from Wheeler, *Voices of 1776,* p. 57.

Elizabeth Bartlett's Letter to a British Officer: adapted from Beard, *America through Women's Eyes,* p. 81.

"Yankee Doodle": adapted from *The Annals of America,* vol. 2, p. 380.

Deborah Champion's Letter to a Friend, 1775: from Beard, *America through Women's Eyes,* p. 73–75.

Phillis Wheatley's "To the Earl of Dartmouth . . .," 1773: from Phillis Wheatley, *Poems on Various Subjects, Religious and Moral* (Walpole, N.H.: David Newhall, 1803; facsimile edition, Boston: Massachusetts Historical Society, 1957), p. 71.

Thomas Paine, *Common Sense,* 1776: adapted from Richard Hofstadter, ed., *Great Issues in American History: From the Revolution to the Civil War, 1765–1865* (New York: Random House, 1958), pp. 53–62.

The Declaration of Independence, 1776: adapted from Cotner et al., *Readings in American History,* vol. 1, pp. 79f.

Dr. Benjamin Rush's Letter to John Adams, 1811: adapted from William J. Bennett, *The Spirit of America* (New York: Simon & Schuster, 1997), pp. 29–30.

Abigail Adams's Letter to John Adams, March 31, 1776: from L. H. Butterfield et al., *The Book of Abigail and John: Selected Letters of the Adams Family, 1762–1764* (Cambridge, Mass.: Harvard University Press, 1975), pp. 120–21.

John Adams's Reply, April 14, 1776: from ibid., pp. 121–22.

Private Joseph Martin's Journal, 1776: from Scheer and Rankin, *Rebels and Redcoats,* p. 181.

Sergeant John Smith's Diary, 1776: adapted from Berger and Berger, *Diary of America,* p. 120.

Sergeant Ezra Lee's Letter to David Humphrey, 1776: adapted from Scheer and Rankin, *Rebels and Redcoats,* pp. 177–78.

Thomas Paine, *The American Crisis,* 1776: from Wheeler, *Voices of 1776,* p. 223.

Colonel John Fitzgerald's Diary, 1776: adapted from Scheer and Rankin, *Rebels and Redcoats,* pp. 211–14.

Diary of Dr. Albigence Waldo, 1777–1778: adapted from Paul M. Angle, *The American Reader* (New York: Rand

McNally, 1958), pp. 111–12.

General Nathaniel Greene's Announcement to the Continental Army, September 16, 1780: from Scheer and Rankin, *Rebels and Redcoats,* p. 384.

James Collins's Journal, 1780: adapted from Wheeler, *Voices of 1776,* p. 356.

James Thacher's Journal, 1781: from Thacher, *Military Journal,* pp. 222–23.

PART VI: Creating a National Government

Abigail Adams's Letter to John Adams, 1776: from King et al., *United States History,* p. 108.

A Farmers' Petition to the State Government, Summer 1786: from Lewis Paul Todd and Merle Curti, *Rise of the American Nation* (New York: Harcourt, 1966), p. 182.

An Interview in the *Massachusetts Centinal,* October 25, 1786: from Linda R. Monk, ed., *Ordinary Americans: U.S. History through the Eyes of Everyday People* (Alexandria, Va.: Close Up Publishing, 1994), p. 35.

Major William Pierce's Notes, 1787: adapted from C. C. Tansill, *Documents Illustrative of the Formation of the Union of the United States* (Washington, D.C.: U.S. Government Printing Office, 1927; reprinted in King et al., *United States History,* p. 28.

A French Visitor's Description of Philadelphia in Summer, 1787: from Catherine Drinker Bowen, *Miracle at Philadelphia* (Boston: Little, Brown, 1986), p. 97.

Patrick Henry's Speech to the Virginia Ratifying Convention, 1788: from Cotner et al., *Readings in American History,* p. 112.

Jonathan Smith's Speech to the Massachusetts Convention, 1788: from Suzanne McIntire, *American Heritage Book of Great American Speeches for Young People* (New York: John Wiley & Sons, 2001), p. 28.

The Constitution, 1788: from *The Constitution of the United States of America* (New York: Barnes & Noble Books, 1987).

The Bill of Rights, Amendments 1–10, 1791: from ibid.

George Washington's Letter to Henry Knox, April 1, 1789: from David Brion Davis and Steven Mintz, *The Boisterous Sea of Liberty: A Documentary History of America from Discovery through the Civil War* (New York: Oxford University Press, 1999), p. 124.

Jonathan Winslow's Diary, April 1789: from *Eyewitness Accounts of the Establishment of the United States of America* (Cooperstown, N.Y.: New York Historical Society, 1967), pp. 88–89.

INDEX